The City of Palaces:
chronicle of a lost heritage

FUNDACIÓN CULTURAL
TELEVISA, A.C.

The City of Palaces: chronicle of a lost heritage, by Guillermo Tovar de Teresa;
1ˢᵗ edition, México, 1990.

©All Rights Reserved, 1ˢᵗ edition, Mexico, 1990, by
Fundación Cultural Televisa, A.C.
Avenida Chapultepec No. 53, 2º piso, Centro, 06720 México, D.F.

Editorial coordination, design & production:

ESPEJO DE OBSIDIANA
EDICIONES

Editorial Coordination: Gabriel Breña Valle
English translation: Bianca Rigoletti and Amy Schildhouse
Edition of English texts: Kieran Maule and Lisa Heller, for Horbach
Language Services, Mexico, D.F.
Graphic Design: Carlos Palmos Olmos
Design Assistant: Braulio Morales Sanchez
Photography: Jose Ignacio Gonzalez Manterola
Associate Photographer: Pablo Oseguera Iturbide
Cartography: Jorge Tamez y Batta
Reconstructive Drawings: Gabriel Breña Valle
Production: Braulio Morales Sanchez and Adriana Arrieta Munguia
Photomechanics, printing and binding: Hindy's, Hong Kong, with
coordination by Jinno International, New York, U.S.A., for
Espejo de Obsidiana, Ediciones, S.A. de C.V. *Printed in Hong Kong*

ISBN:968-6258-08-6   Complete Work
ISBN:968-6258-10-8   Volume II

Guillermo Tovar de Teresa
Chronicler of Mexico City

The City of Palaces:
chronicle of a lost heritage

Introductory texts
Enrique Krauze
José Iturriaga

Volume II

Vuelta

Mexico, 1990

Photography Credits

The photographic material in this book belongs to the following collections:

Culhuacan Library, National Institute of Anthropology and History/National Council on Arts and Culture, Mexico

8, 11, 12, 16, 17, 18 ab., 18 bel., 19 ab., 20, 21 ab., 22, 23 ab., 23 bel., 27 ab., 35 bel., 40 ab., 42 ab., 44 ab., 44 bel., 53 ab., 53 bel., 57, 58, 64 ab., 66 ab., 66 bel., 70, 71 ab., 74 ab., 76 ab., 79, 82, 88 bel., 91, 100 bel., 104, 105, 106 ab., 108, 109 ab., 115 ab., 116 ab., 119, 120 ab., 128 ab., 137 bel., 141 ab., 141 bel., 142 right, 143, 144 ab., 145, 146 ab., 146 bel., 147, 150 ab., 150 bel., 151, 152 ab., 154 ab., 156 ab., 156 bel., 157 bel., 159, 160 ab., 162 bel., 164 ab., 165, 166 ab., 166 bel., 167 ab., 167 bel., 168 ab., 170 ab., 171 right, 172 ab., 175 ab., 177, 178, 180 ab., 181 ab., 182 ab., 184 ab., 184 bel., 185 ab.

National Viceregal Museum, National Institute of Anthropology and History/National Council on Arts and Culture, Mexico

162 ab.

Manuel Orozco y Berra Map Library, Secretariat of Hydraulic Resources

14, 72 ab., 176 ab.

Photographic Archives of National School of Professional Studies/National Autonomous University of Mexico

50 bel., 67 bel., 84, 118, 134 ab., 135, 136 ab., 136 bel., 138, 139, 140.

Notarial Archives of the Federal District

100 ab., 101 ab., 113 ab., 122.

Guillermo Tovar de Teresa

24, 27 bel., 28, 30 ab., 31 bel., 32 bel., 33 ab., 34 ab., 34 bel., 35 ab., 38 ab., 43 ab., 46 ab., 48 ab., 48 bel., 49 left, 52, 54 ab., 56, 67 ab., 69 ab., 76 bel., 77 ab., 80 ab., 86 ab., 87, 88 ab., 89 ab., 89 bel., 90 ab., 92 ab., 92 right, 92 left., 93 ab., 94 ab., 95 left, 96 ab., 97 left., 98 ab., 99, 102 ab., 103, 107, 112, 124 ab., 125, 126, 132 ab., 132 bel., 133 ab., 133 bel., 158, 163 ab., 169, 171 left

Jose Ignacio Conde

19 bel., 26, 30 bel., 31 ab., 32 ab., 36 ab., 39 left, 47, 50 ab., 59 ab., 60 ab., 61, 62, 68., 74 bel., 110 ab., 111, 114, 123, 127, 142 left, 173, 174.

All these photographs have been reproduced by OG Fotografos, S.C. for Espejo de Obsidiana, Ediciones, S.A. de C.V. with permission of the copyright holders.

The modern photographs were taken *ex profeso* for this first edition by Jose Ignacio Gonzalez Manterola, with the collaboration of Pablo Oseguera

21 ab., 25, 29, 33 ab., 37 ab., 38 ab., 39 der., 42 ab., 43 ab., 45, 49 der., 51, 59 ab., 60 ab., 63 arr., 69 ab., 71 ab., 75, 77 ab., 78 arr., 85, 93 ab., 95 der., 97 der., 104-105, 109 ab., 115 ab., 117, 129, 130 arr., 131, 137 arr., 148, 153, 157 arr., 161, 163 ab., 175 ab., 179, 181 ab., 185 ab.

Table of Contents

	Page
DIAGRAM OF MEXICO CITY	6
VIII CONVENTS FOR FRIARS	9
Great O.H.F. Francisco de Mexico Convent	13
Santa Cruz de Tlatelolco College	37
Convent of O.H.F. Diego, of the Barefoot Religious Followers of O.H.F. Francisco	41
Old Propaganda Fide de San Fernando College	47
Imperial Santo Domingo de Mexico Convent	55
San Agustin Convent	65
Nuestra Señora de las Mercedes Convent, redemption of the Imprisoned	73
Nuestra Señora de Monserrat	79
La Casa Profesa of the Society of Jesus	81
IX CONVENTS FOR NUNS	83
La Concepcion	87
The Royal Monastery of Jesus Maria	91
La Encarnacion	95
Santa Ines	97
Balvanera	99
San Jose de Gracia	103
San Bernardo	107
Santa Clara	111
San Juan de la Penitencia	117
Santa Isabel	121
Capuchinas	125
Corpus Christi	129
San Lorenzo	131
Santa Catalina de Siena	135
Santa Teresa La Antigua	143
Santa Brigida	145
X HOSPITALS AND SCHOOLS	149
Jesus Hospital	153
San Andres and Santa Paula	155
Betlemitas	161
Real de Naturales Hospital	165
Hospice for the Poor	169
Espiritu Santo Hospital	171
Terceros Hospital	173
Girls School	177
San Ramon College	181
Jesuit Schools	183
CONCLUSION	187
ONOMASTIC INDEX	190

Diagram of Mexico City

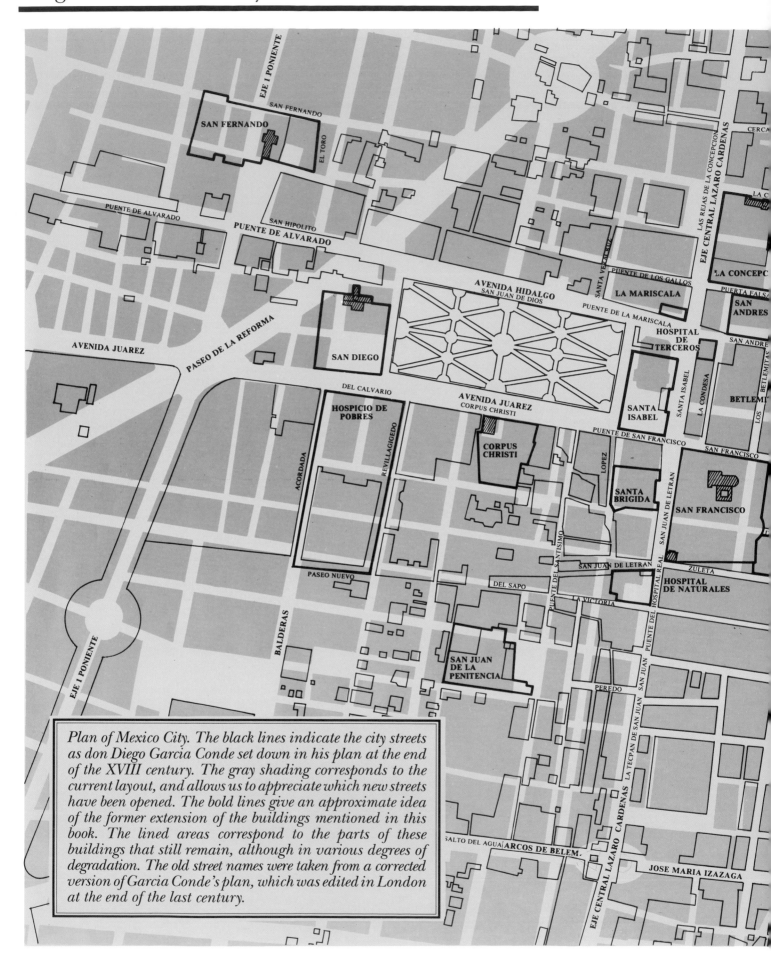

Plan of Mexico City. The black lines indicate the city streets as don Diego García Conde set down in his plan at the end of the XVIII century. The gray shading corresponds to the current layout, and allows us to appreciate which new streets have been opened. The bold lines give an approximate idea of the former extension of the buildings mentioned in this book. The lined areas correspond to the parts of these buildings that still remain, although in various degrees of degradation. The old street names were taken from a corrected version of García Conde's plan, which was edited in London at the end of the last century.

VIII Convents for Friars

MEXICO CITY'S HISTORY is intimately linked to the three religious orders that were first established in New Spain: the Franciscans as of 1523, with the presence of Brothers Pedro de Gante, Juan de Tecto and Juan de Aora and later with the first twelve in 1524; the Dominicans, from 1526 and, the Augustinians in 1533. Upon their arrival in the city, they founded their orders in key locations.

There has been a great deal of debate about the place that the Franciscans chose for the old San Francisco Church yet, the fact is that from very early on, they decided to settle just where they have been for more than four hundred years. The Dominicans and the Augustinians were located on opposite sides of the Main Square. Consequently, the distance between them was considerable: San Francisco to the west, Santo Domingo to the north and San Agustin to the south. The city plan was extended during Viceroy Antonio de Mendoza's years in government (1535-1550), an example of which is the construction of the Augustine Church, that was built after the streets leading to it had been laid out. Information on the early years of these buildings can be found in the Mercedes section of the General Archives of the Nation and the City Hall Records. They were later rebuilt and expanded as chapels were constructed in their atriums, land was acquired or donated and new buildings were erected.

A new stage in the life of the city began during the second half of the XVI century. Viceroy Mendoza's successor, Viceroy Luis de Velazco was aware of the need for an extremely competent master architect. Claudio de Arciniega arrived from Spain for this purpose and, after completing various works in Puebla, came to Mexico City, where he undertook several construction projects. At a later date, he was the master craftsman of architecture in the Mexico City Cathedral and the designer of its plan. He carried out works on the *De Profundis* room in the San Francisco Church and arranged the Cervantes family grave. He also built the San Agustin and Santo Domingo churches. The latter, according to the Cathedral's canon, Doctor don Sancho Muñon (1585), ''since the year of fifteen hundred and fifty three when it was begun, to the end of fifteen hundred and eighty four, it cost two hundred and sixty two thousand two hundred and fifty three pesos, three tomins and four grains of the so-called common gold'', in other words, a fortune.

A considerable amount of information is available on these buildings and will be included in the respective chapters. Nevertheless, we would like to underline their importance since none of this remains. It was mentioned that

Old San Diego Novitiate. Lithograph dating from the mid XIX century.

Convents for Friars

in the second half of the XVI century, and with the arrival of Arciniega, Becerra and other great architects, the city's buildings underwent a metamorphosis: primitive constructions were replaced by magnificent buildings with Plateresque frontispieces and a new physiognomy that was more in keeping with the Renaissance spirit.

The Jesuits arrived around 1572 and found lodging in the San Agustin Convent. Father Pedro Sanchez befriended the prior, Brother Juan Adriano, and together they decided to organize poetry competitions. Later, around 1580-1585, when the Jesuits decided to establish their Casa Profesa, they encountered many difficulties; firstly, they had no land in the central part of the city and, secondly, the other religious orders -including the Augustinians- were opposed to their neighbors due to the existence of a Pontifical grant protecting them, which prevented new orders from constructing buildings in an area of 180 and 300 "canas" (1 "cana" equals 2.23 meters) around them. Their interests were consequently protected, especially those relating to alms and donations. They attempted to solve this complicated dispute by settling on the corner of San Sebastian and Oidores streets, on land obtained by Father Pedro Mercado who came from a family of Conquistadores. The Franciscans and the Dominicans -the Augustinians less- protested vigorously due to the fact that their territories were being invaded (all this is registered in the city government records). An agreement was finally reached and, as a result, their church and exercise house were built. The Jesuits were interested in having a good location, in the wealthy part of the city, in order to be able to influence the elite. Nevertheless, their Magno Colegio de San Pedro y San Pablo had to be situated a long way off, in the eastern part of the city.

Those belonging to the Merced (1582) and Carmelite (1585) orders ran into the same complications. The former, of Guatemalan origin, did not get its novitiate and school until 1593. The others had to initially go to the San Sebastian hermitage and from there on to another place, almost on the city limits in the present day El Carmen Square.

The Hospitalers orders were established and, little by little, the number of convents in the city grew. The clergymen dressed in habits of different colors, were, in themselves, a significant population.

The friars convents were veritable citadels. Different parts of the population went to them to form confraternities and brotherhoods. In San Fernando, for example, the meeting place for the members of the Merchants Council was formed; the Basques installed themselves in the Aranzazu Chapel, those from Rioja in the Balvanera Chapel and the ones from Santander in the Señor de Burgos Chapel. Next to the main church was the Purisima Concepcion Chapel, called Zuleta or Del Consulado, after its prior, Captain Pedro de Zuleta. In addition, there was also the Los Naturales Chapel which later belonged to the Servites, and the Tercer Orden Chapel. In Santo Domingo and La Merced there were chapels for "colored people", and in every convent there were much-worshipped images that became extremely popular: in San Agustin, the *Totolapan Christ*; Santo Domingo possessed an image of the same saint, bearing the Neapolitan name of *Soriano*, which provided much comfort during the years of the flood. San Francisco housed the remains of Brother Antonio Margil de Jesus, the so-called "Northern Pilgrim" and evangelist of Texas who, though not a titular saint, had a sort of cult

View of the Santo Domingo Square, oil on canvas (c.1840). This rare painting shows us the square in its full splendor, while the influence of Pedro Arrieta, the designer of the church, the porter's lodge of the old Inquisicion Palace and of the old Customs House or Mexico City Merchants Council, was still apparent. Fortunately, it can be said that Santo Domingo is the best conserved square in Mexico City.

following. The Jesuits had a great wealth of relics and when they arrived in Mexico, they built triumphal arches in honor of these bones.

The orders had their own schools. Tlatelolco, a famous foundation that still exists, although its church was looted, owes its existence to the efforts made by Franciscan Brother Juan de Torquemada at the end of the XVI century and the beginning of the XVII. The Dominicans had the San Pablo School, and the Jesuits, the San Pedro y San Pablo and the San Gregorio schools. Around 1576, the Dieguinos, who were actually barefoot Franciscans, passed through New Spain on their way to the Philippines and some of them stayed on, founding their novitiate and convent in 1591. In other cases, the novitiates were also in the city. The Hospitalers had wonderful buildings until they were suppressed in 1820. The inventories of these buildings can still be found in the old Temporalities section of the General Archives of the Nation. I find the Bethlemites School impressive because of the large amount of furniture and paintings that it contained.

In conclusion, these religious buildings, which are now partially destroyed, damaged or razed, were an important part of the life of the capital, giving the city a physiognomy and, in some cases, enriching its nomenclature. Of all of these buildings, not one is still intact.

In the following pages we shall take a glance at the friar's convents, providing information on their artistic tradition, and relating the extent of their destruction. Our aim is not to record the history of each of them, but rather to point out the parts of them that no longer exist.

Aranzazu Chapel. Photograph taken around 1860. This chapel was removed at the end of the XIX century, to make way for yet another temple, the San Felipe de Jesus Church. The only thing that was salvaged from this church was the inscription on the upper entablature.

The Great O.H.F. Francisco de Mexico Convent

SUPPOSEDLY, THERE ONCE WAS a simple church called San Francisco in the place where the first Cathedral of Mexico was built. According to this version, the Franciscans decided to move to a place closer to the Indian population, across from the city's western canals. Here, they would have an enormous piece of land, adequate for the church, the Indians' chapel and the convent. It well may have been this way, and the energetic Brother Pedro de Gante probably did arrange his school for the Indians within the enormous atrium of his convent. At the outset, the church was quite modest and, although it was later rebuilt, in 1554, Cervantes de Salazar described it as insufficient. This would explain why, when the funeral rites for Carlos V were arranged, they were not held in the church, but rather in Los Naturales Chapel.

A new church was built in 1590. Torquemada provides some information about it, such as his comments on the excellence of the main altarpiece, donated by don Francisco de Heredia at a cost of fourteen thousand pesos. It had sixteen magnificent sculptures and panels by a famed artist, perhaps Echave Orio, who around this period, painted the Tlatelolco Altarpiece and was a neighbor of San Francisco Street.

As time went by, the church was enriched until it was ruined by sinking almost a full four "varas". Vetancourt points out that the burial of Hernan Cortes, adorned with a canopy, his weapons and his portrait, along with the graves of several knights and conquerors, was on the gospel transept. The main altarpiece was no longer the one described by Torquemada, but rather one by Pedro Ramirez and Basilio Salazar, with its imitation Jasper socle, four painted streets and five sculpted ones, and magnificent sagrarium. It was also adorned with a great sculpture of *San Francisco* standing on a globe of the world held up by four angels, the polychromed *Purisima Concepcion* on a gilt background, the Calvario, sixteen statues of saints and panel paintings.

The altarpiece cost fourteen thousand pesos and was made under the supervision of Brother Mateo de Heredia, who was a relative of the donor, don Francisco de Heredia. The contract for the work mentions San Francisco's diadem and the Virgin's crown, both made of silver, and the old altarpiece that sculptor and assembler Pedro Ramirez would have to remove. The church was demolished in 1710. In 1628, the Purisima Concepcion Chapel, donated by Captain Zuleta, was built next to it. The roofing on this chapel was coffered wood, the work of gilder Pedro de la Cruz and plasterer Diego Lopez Morillo. The contract states that "all the loops must be gilded, some in burnished gold and the blue enamel fields and the fronts and end walls will have matte gold fleurons".

Convents for Friars

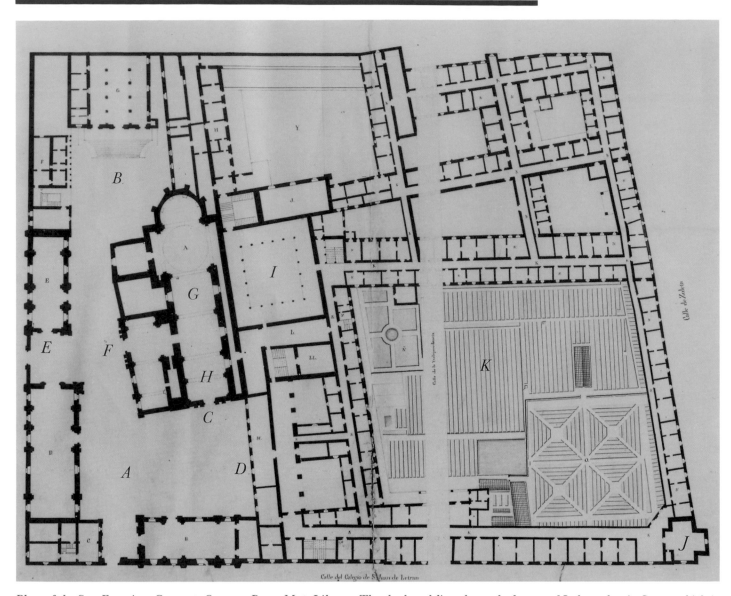

Plan of the San Francisco Convent, Orozco y Berra Map Library. The shadowed line shows the layout of Independencia Street, which is currently one of the sections of 16 de Septiembre Street. It is interesting to compare this relatively unknown document with the plan published by Antonio Garcia Cubas in his book My Book of Memoirs, *which is a remarkable source of information on Mexico City during the mid XIX century. If other plans of the city's convents had survived, as this one did, we would at least have an exact idea of all that has been lost. The letters that have been added, mark different points within this enormous convent: A) Atrium; B) Servitas Chapel; C) Frontispiece of the main church; D) Porter's Lodge; E) Aranzazu Chapel; F) Balvanera Chapel; G) Main Church; H) Choir; I) Large Cloister; J) San Antonio Chapel; and K) Orchard.*

Among the XVII century treasures of San Francisco were two silver frontals made by craftsman Miguel Ruiz Parra in 1657, and a liturgical service - chalices, patens chrismatories, etcetera - made by Alonso Paris in 1663. With regard to the altarpieces, there was one, the *Santo Despedimento*, the work of Francisco Arjona Montalvo, which was moved to Los Naturales Chapel. The artist, an associate of Andres de Fuentes, also created the *Culhuacan* altarpiece and a side piece for the Tercer Orden de San Francisco Chapel. Antonio Maldonado did two lateral pieces for the church: one, on the left hand side of the Consulado Chapel, dedicated to *Nuestra Señora de la Aurora* (1673), and the other, which also no longer exists, that served as the tomb of the rector of Christ College.

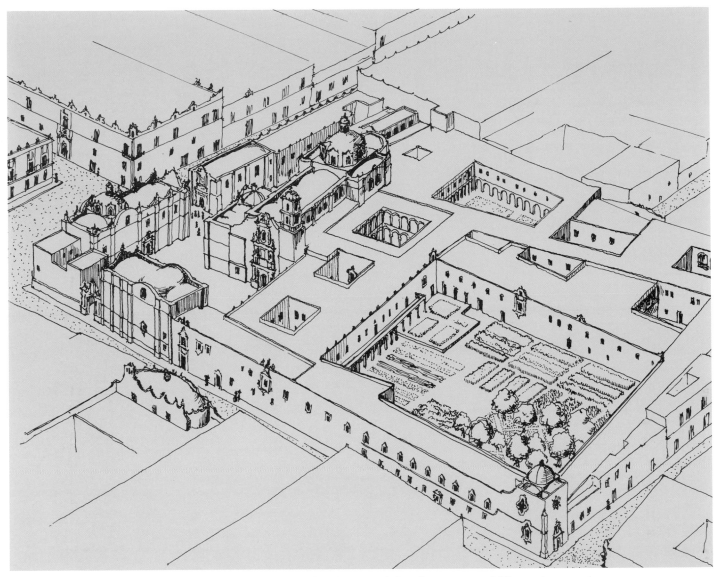

Hypothetical reconstruction of the San Francisco Convent, based on remaining documents and illustrations.

The old convent was rebuilt in the XVI and XVII centuries. We have information from diarist Antonio de Robles that in 1701, the 1649 cloister was redone. As described by chronicler Vetancourt, this building underwent a Baroque transformation under Juan Antonio de la Cruz and stonecutter Antonio de Rojas. It was decorated with paintings by Baltazar de Echave.

During the middle of the XVII century, the San Francisco Convent had an imposing appearance. The Tercer Orden Chapel possessed an altarpiece by Pedro Maldonado; that of San Jose de los Españoles was very sumptuous. Los Naturales Chapel was rich in altarpieces, and its tower was even higher than that of the main church. The Viacrucis Chapels were distributed all along the old Calvario Highway, today Juarez Avenue. Those of the first and second stations, built by architect Marco Antonio Sobrarias, due to the patronage of famous university chronicler don Cristobal de la Plaza y Jaen, were inside the convent.

As we have already mentioned, the convent was rebuilt once again during the XVIII century, as were almost all of its chapels. The main church was

Convents for Friars

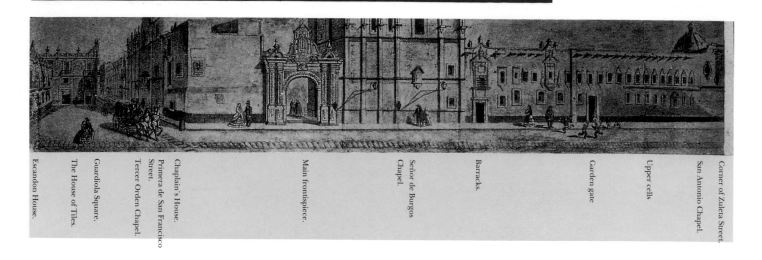

Escandon House.
The House of Tiles.
Guardiola Square.
Primera de San Francisco Street.
Tercer Orden Chapel.
Chaplain's House.
Main frontispiece.
Señor de Burgos Chapel.
Barracks.
Garden gate.
Upper cells.
San Antonio Chapel.
Corner of Zuleta Street.

rebuilt and opened in 1716. Its main altarpiece was the work of Mateo de Pinos. At the end of the XVIII century, it was replaced by another magnificent one by Jeronimo Antonio Gil. It is the same one that we are familiar with through the lithographs and the map made by this academic artist. The choir stalls were the work of Juan de Rojas, the same craftsman who built those of the Cathedral. The architects that oversaw the work were Feliciano Cabello and Jose de los Santos. These and other details can be consulted in the magnificent study made on this building by Eduardo Baen, who consulted the builders' book that is preserved in the University of Texas at Austin Library, as a source for his study.

The Tercer Orden Chapel was rebuilt by Pedro de Arrieta, which caused him a serious problem, because he did not do the work the way that the Tertiaries expected it. Consequently, it was necessary to ask ten of the city's architects for expert advice. The chapel was finally opened in 1732. Its main altarpiece was the work of Jeronimo de Balbas, who also created the one in San Jose. The former is perhaps one of the basic "Estipite" Baroque works and the one that most influenced other craftsmen. It served as a model for the Santa Catarina main altarpiece (1737) by Felipe Ureña, which in turn, provided the inspiration for the one in Tepotzotlan, by Higinio Chavez and Miguel Cabrera (1753). Thanks to this last altarpiece, we can imagine the model, which was lost forever, as were all those in the Tercer Orden Chapel. We should recall the lavish Jesuit interior of Tepotzotlan in order to imagine the luxuriance of this chapel, which aside from the aforementioned Balbas altarpieces, also had other altarpieces done by Ureña between 1739 and 1740.

The interior of the XVII century Aranzazu Chapel was renovated in the final years of the following century, although Neoclassic altarpieces were used. The exterior of the Balvanera Chapel, which was built between 1763 and 1766, was congruent with its interior, and both were extremely ornate as they were made at the height of "Estipite" Baroque. The chapel of the Servites, thus named because they were "the Virgin's servants", was the last redoubt of the impressive San Jose de los Naturales Chapel, which had seven naves and was comparable only to the one in Cholula. It was opened in 1791. The San Antonio Chapel, on the corner of Zuleta, today Venustiano Carranza Avenue, was the work of Miguel Jose de Rivera and was opened in 1740.

Western facade of the San Francisco Convent, as seen from present day Madero Street to Venustiano Carranza Avenue. With the exception of the San Francisco Chapel in the south corner, nothing of this group remains (mid XIX century).

16

Guardiola Square as depicted by Casimiro Castro (c.1855). Thanks to this lithograph, we can see the part of the convent at the corner of old San Francisco Street (today Madero Street) and San Juan de Letran Street. As we can appreciate, the facade facing north belonged to the house of the Tercer Orden Chaplain, the doorway leading to the atrium (which is still preserved), the Aranzazu Chapel, the Chaplain of Aranzazu's house and the wall that enclosed the Servita's Garden. The old house of the Marquis de Santa Fe de Guardiola could be seen across the way.

According to Ignacio Carrillo y Perez' description in *Catholic, Genteel and Political Mexico*, the San Francisco Convent was truly magnificent. According to Father Fidel Chauvet, the last person to own this now lost manuscript, was don Federico Gomez de Orozco. Carillo described the entire building and gave detailed information on its conditions, shortly before it suffered its first destruction at the hands of Neoclassic fury.

In order to give the reader an idea of what this distinguished convent once was, we have provided the map from the Orozco y Berra Map Library. If it were not for this map and the one published by Garcia Cubas, in conjunction with his and Ramirez de Aparicio's descriptions, we would have no more than our imagination to evoke it and be surprised by its immensity, having housed so many buildings.

Convents for Friars

Here we see the demolition of the street corner which appears intact in the Casimiro Castro lithograph. It is clear how the Tercer Orden Chapel and the gatekeeper's cell have been torn down. It also depicts the destruction of the main facade of the large church, which was "scraped" to turn it into a smooth wall, so as to facilitate construction beside it. This 1861 lithograph is part of a period calendar.

The Casa de los Azulejos was preserved, as we can see in this circa 1800 lithograph, depicting the transformation of the site. In the place of the provincial Franciscan priest's house, the Botica Nueva on the ground floor.

Above, the San Francisco atrium viewed from west to east. To the left, the Tercer Orden Chapel, in the rear, the Aranzazu Chapel; in the background, the Servitas Chapel. In the center, on one side of the main church, the Balvanera Chapel appears. To the left, we can see the portico, which, I suppose is from the same period as the Balvanera Chapel and which had paintings depicting the life of Sebastian de Aparicio. The library was on the second floor (1853 Watercolor). Below, the demolition of the Servitas Chapel. Could these columns be those very old ones that came from the San Jose de los Naturales Chapel? The great work of Brother Pedro de Gante was built here during the XVI century.

Convents for Friars

Frontispiece and portal of the main church. Photograph taken around 1855. This unique image, discovered by Francisco de la Maza in San Luis Potosi, allows us to appreciate the exterior of this destroyed church, with its Arrieta-style portico, made under the direction of Feliciano Cabello and Jose de los Santos between 1714 and 1716. The portal archways were adorned with lambrequin on the spandrels and the voussoirs were carved with figures of saints. The upper floor was made of volcanic and Chiluca stone.

Above, the window of the old San Francisco de Mexico Convent Doorway. This photograph from the nineteen forties shows the portal still in existence, and the little that remained intact after the Reform, was destroyed by the avarice of real estate brokers.

To the right, the doorway in its present state. It is the only remnant of a building that was demolished as a consequence of the 1985 earthquakes. Note that the second floor windows were rebuilt.

Convents for Friars

View of the old San Francisco Arcade that was turned into a billiards hall during the nineteen twenties. The original archways are still preserved, even though the ornaments of the lambrequins and the figures on the keystones of the arches have been damaged.

Roof of the structure belonging to the billiards hall shown in the previous photograph. The tower and the socle of the main body of the can belfry also be appreciated. We can clearly see how the Rule building was constructed up against the wall, where the principal frontispiece of the main church once was. A volute from the finial of the razed frontispiece can just barely be seen here.

Demolition of the old San Francisco Arcade. The existing archway is not the original one. (c.1955)

The Balvanera Chapel around 1855. This masterpiece of the Churrigueresque style of New Spain could have been saved had it not fallen into the hands of Monsigneur Riley, an iconoclast who removed all the ornamental figures, including the panel depicting the stigmatization of San Francisco, the figures in the vaulted niches, the reliefs on the balustered columns and even the numerous little angels and cherubs.

The main altarpiece of the Santa Catalina Church, which will be discussed later, was moved to this chapel.

This magnificent 1855 lithograph, taken from the newspaper, La Cruz, shows us the full splendor of the magnificent main altarpiece by Jeronimo Antonio Gil (1872), a superb example of Neoclassicism in New Spain.

Interior of the large San Francisco de Mexico Church. Although the decorative style was Neoclassic, the interior still had an extremely majestic air. 1853 watercolor.

Interior of the San Francisco Church shortly after it was looted and devastated (1862). This interesting photograph shows how the rich interior of the Franciscan Church ended up as a coach house and stable.

The same interior around 1880, when the building was used as a Protestant church.

The San Francisco Church was returned to the Catholic religion, and the Franciscans made a great effort to reproduce the original altarpiece.

Convents for Friars

This 1880 photograph shows the choir completely empty.

Below, the San Francisco choir in a lithograph by Iriarte (1862). The magnificent choir stalls, the work of Juan de Rojas (1715), were turned into firewood.

The door leading to the large San Francisco Church Choir. As we can see, it also acted as the cover design of a beautiful book, one of the few that dealt with the artistic tragedy which the destruction of these convents implied.

The side of the San Francisco Convent, photographed from the roof of the home of the Marquis de Santa Fe de Guardiola. In the foreground, the courtyard can be seen and, further back on the left, the Count de Valle de Orizaba's Palace, better known as the House of Tiles.
In the background the dome of the large San Francisco Church appears. On the right, the Baroque profile of the Tercer Orden Chapel and part of its dome are outlined.

Convents for Friars

Above, the San Francisco Cloister (Iriarte, 1862). Note how the corridor floor is being torn up. To the left, the San Antonio Chapel. This building was described in the **Mexico Gazette** *on the day of its inauguration in 1740. The work of Miguel Jose de Rivera, this building narrowly missed being demolished as was the adjacent Cook building, which was partially supported by the old convent's walls and galleries. It finally disappeared during the nineteen sixties, and as yet, nothing has been built to take its place.*

The same cloister in the nineteen twenties, converted into a Protestant church. It was thanks to this that the building was saved from the clutches of a speculator who would have demolished it.

This chapel has been restored, and its conservation would seem to be assured. Construction of a large building was begun on the land behind it, and any traces of the Franciscan Convent that might have remained were thus erased. It is still unfinished.

The two photographs on the opposite page depict the orchard of the San Francisco de Mexico Convent. Since before the Reform, the friars no longer occupied the entire convent. Around 1855, one part was already used as a barracks, and the orchard was leased and later awarded to Frenchman Constancio Tonel. The orchards and convent buildings that were on that property were turned into the Hotel Jardín in 1886. Its owner was Romualdo Zamora y Duque. The convent refectory was to the east of the garden, and at the end of the last century, it was used as the sitting room for Juan Galant's boarding house. Photographs from 1886.

Above right, a photograph from approximately 1856, showing how the convent was razed when the street was opened up. The scene looks like a bomb site. According to Garcia Cubas, a presidential decree of September of the same year, ordered the building's destruction a few days after a group of people were unjustly accused of treason and apprehended inside the convent. The government had to demagogically harangue the workers until they finally agreed to tear down the walls of this venerable construction.

The photograph below shows the opening of Independencia Street in 1856. Lithograph from the era, taken from a calendar. It was also used to illustrate the cover of a Polish polka composed for piano by J. Perez de Leon entitled, Independence Street and was part of a collection called Memories of the San Francisco Convent.

Convents for Friars

Detail of the Tlatelolco Franciscan Church, from an 1862 lithograph.

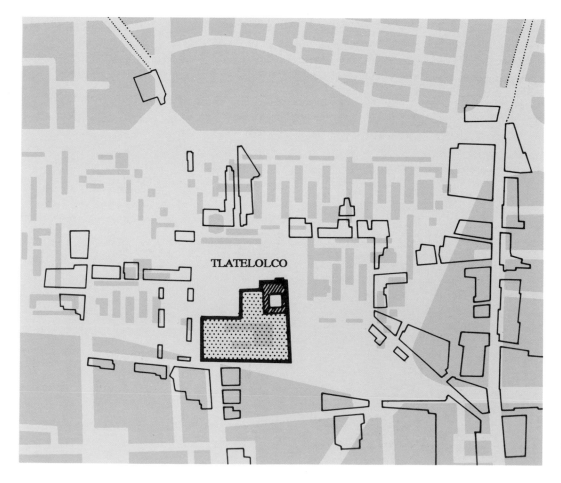

TLATELOLCO

The Tlatelolco Convent surrounded by the buildings and spaces of the housing complex.

The Santa Cruz de Tlatelolco College

THE STORY of the Santa Cruz de Tlatelolco College, founded by Brother Juan de Zumarraga and Viceroy Antonio de Mendoza around 1543, is very well known, since the purpose of this celebrated school was to teach its students three languages. It consequently had an excellent library of Latin texts that included works by Virgil, Pedro Apiano, Plato and others, as well as the Erasmus version of the gospel according to Saint Hieronymite.

At the end of the XVI century, the church was rebuilt thanks to the efforts of Brother Juan de Torquemada. He decided that indigenous sculptors and assemblers from Tlatelolco would build the main altarpiece, the paintings of which would be the work of the Basque, Baltazar de Echave Orio.

The school was rebuilt in the XVII century, around 1660. Franciscan Juan de la Torre, Bishop of Nicaragua, encouraged the building of the cloister, the cells, the library and even a refectory for one hundred friars. The convent then came under the guardianship of don Pedro de Soto Lopez. The school was reopened in 1667 under the name San Buenaventura. In the "Gomez de Orozco" fund of the General Archives of the Nation, there is an inventory of the library, which was made around 1663. It had 720 titles and included the old volumes contained in the library, one of the oldest in America. This collection survived, enriched with new titles, until the XIX century, when it was looted, and almost all of its volumes were acquired by the bookseller Abadiano who sold them to Sutro who in turn, took them to California where they remain.

The same detail as the one on the opposite page, Saint John the Evangelist, riding an eagle, the animal that symbolizes him.

Rear view of the church and convent in the mid XIX century. The building was used as a garrison, a jail for political prisoners and even as a warehouse.

The gatekeeper's lodge behind the church was added on a few decades ago, salvaging it from another building that has since disappeared.

To the left, the interior of the Franciscan Tlatelolco Church, as depicted in a lithograph by Iriarte (1862). The main altarpiece, dating from the late XVI century, was reduced to dust. Some of the paintings were rescued thanks to Jose Bernardo Couto, who obtained them from the friars by exchanging the originals for copies made by students of the San Carlos Academy. Couto chose the originals and had them set aside for a museum that he planned to open. The students' copies and other paintings from the altarpiece disappeared along with the columns, reliefs, figures of saints and the other lateral pieces, such as the fabulous San Antonio, that was so widely commented upon in many issues of the Mexico Gazette. *All of this destruction was carried out to turn the church into a railway warehouse. It was truly a miracle when, in the fifties, the relief of Santiago Apostol appeared. As we can see in the photograph at right, this is all that remains of the art produced by viceregal carvers. It now adorns the barren apse of the church.*

Convents for Friars

Kitchen of the San Diego Convent. Mid XIX century lithograph.

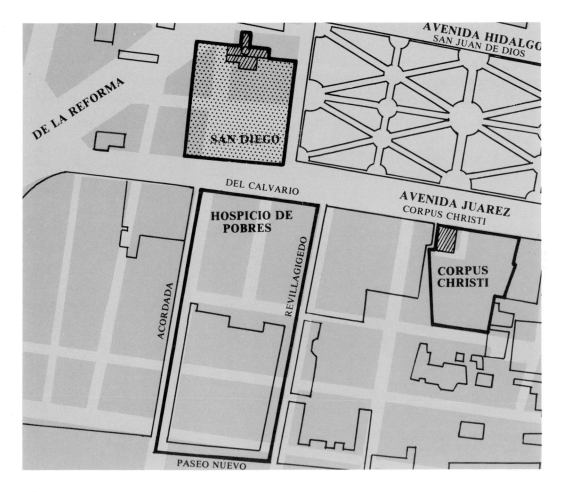

Location of the San Diego Convent. The street that once separated it from Alameda Park is now called Doctor Mora. The name El Calvario, on what is now Juarez Avenue, is reminiscent of some of the chapels that were built there and visited during the Holy Week procession. Part of what once was the convent is now Solidarity Square.

Convent of O.H.F. Diego of the Barefoot Religious Followers of O.H.F. Francisco

THE SAN DIEGO DE MEXICO CONVENT, built in front of Alameda Park, was sponsored by Don Mateo Mauleon at the beginning of the XVII century. The patronage was inherited, and given the peculiar circumstance of it having been the private property of its patrons, the convent was also inherited.

Every year, a ceremony was held in the San Diego Convent, in which the patrons received the keys to the convent and symbolically returned them to the friars. The patronage eventually belonged to the Counts del Valle de Orizaba, and the last Count -who accompanied Empress Charlotte to Rome- signed it over to his cousin Andres Davis, the son of an Englishman and the last Mariscala of Castille. This priest decided to divide the land into plots, because he was afraid of government reprisals. As of 1867, he sold off the lots that made up the orchard, the novitiate and the convent.

At the end of the XVIII century, the church had an extremely somber exterior and was reconstructed in 1778. In the course of the same year, the Dolores Chapel was built, and the church boasted two beautiful cupolas.

In the mid XIX century the exterior was renovated again and the Classic style imposed. A lithograph and a watercolor, done in 1847 and 1850 respectively, still remain, in which the old atrium wall and the bull's eyes of the chapel windows are depicted. Consequently, the newly renovated convent reached the years of the Reform.

The interior altarpieces disappeared when the above-mentioned repairs were carried out. Nevertheless, the convent was rich in paintings and books. The tomb of the Valle de Orizaba family was located somewhere in the building; it was covered with magnificent tiles that were adorned with the family coat-of-arms. When this part of the convent disappeared, the tiles were taken to the home of the Counts del Valle de Orizaba and displayed on the staircase.

While discussing the San Diego Convent, I would like to point out that Couto mentioned having seen a Saint Anthony of Padua with the Child, by Luis Juarez, dating from 1610, in the convent. He took it to the San Carlos Academy, but it disappeared, because it can no longer be found in the Vice-regal Pinacotheca collection, composed of the paintings of New Spain that were the property of the Academy and which were kept in San Diego itself.

San Diego has been partially preserved. A section of the convent, the church and the Dolores Chapel are now used for the Viceregal Pinacotheca. The rest was turned into a parking lot, an electrical substation and an office building, and the novitiate became a restaurant. The orchard disappeared. Fortunately, there is currently a project to restore the complex, thanks to the Architecture Division of the National Fine Arts Institute.

Above, this 1930 photograph shows the San Diego Cloister before it was turned into the Viceregal Pinacotheca. It was destroyed in order to build a parking lot.
To the left, the section of the cloister that was rescued from destruction and designated for the museum.

The above photograph shows Los Dolores Chapel. The efforts to keep it in vogue have led to the disappearance of its viceregal decoration. It is not even certain that the oil paintings are from the XIX century.

On the right, a current view of the chapel. The mural in the background, which is the work of Federico Cantu, extols the virtue of the Franciscans' labors in New Spain.

Convents for Friars

An 1847 lithograph drawn to show a movable trench that was built to defend the city during the war with the United States. Fortunately, it also captures the image of the old San Diego Convent in its original state.

An 1853 watercolor showing San Diego after one of the changes it underwent.

It seems that the preservation of the remains of the San Diego Convent is assured. We cannot say the same for its inexorably changing surroundings.

Convents for Friars

Orchard hot house at the San Fernando Convent in 1855.

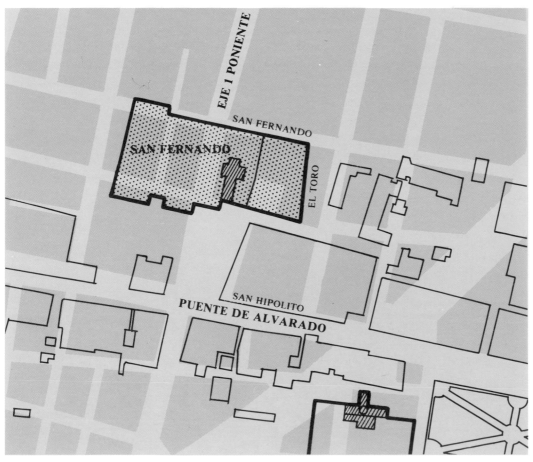

The location of the San Fernando Convent. The name San Fernando still exists, though not on the street behind the convent, which is now known as Mina Street, but rather, on the one in front. When the street dividing the convent was laid, it was called Guerrero, but it has since been supplanted by Western Thoroughfare 1.

Old Propaganda Fide de San Fernando College

THE EVANGELIZATION OF TEXAS is linked to the miraculous Queretaro Cross because, in 1570, many members of the order that were passing through Queretaro with Fernando de Tapia, the Conqueror, built their convent on the spot where the Cross was located. This building was later abandoned and in 1643, the members of the religious order decided to establish a collection house there, which was carried out in 1666. Brother Antonio Linaz obtained a papal bull which allowed him to establish a school with twenty-two missionaries. Consequently, the Propaganda Fide de Queretaro College was established.

In 1730, these missionaries wished to found a house in Mexico. A year later, they purchased the land and the orchard from don Agustin de Oliva and built a hospice that would later serve as a school and convent. In 1735, the first stone for the new church was laid, and in April, 1755, the church was opened. At some point during the construction of the church, around 1738, the work was directed by Jeronimo de Balbas. At a later date, Antonio Alvarez and Eduardo Herrera took his place.

The building was severely damaged by an earthquake in 1858. In December, 1860, the complex was disentailed. The church was completely sacked; its elegant Churrigueresque altarpieces by Jose Joaquin de Sayago, disappeared; the library was scattered, the church towers lost their bells, and the convent was divided into three lots. At the beginning of the century, the choir stalls were removed and taken to the then Guadalupe Collegiate Church; it was left with Neoclassic altarpieces and some decorations on the cupola and in the vaults. This decor was also destroyed a few years ago, in order to make way for a newly-made pilaster altarpiece that makes us long for the old gilding of the lateral pieces. The convent was destroyed in the nineteen thirties, when it was still in fairly good condition. The paintings by Jose de Paez that adorned the cloister were rescued by Brother Luis de Refugio Palacio, who took them to Zapopan, where they remain to this day. The deterioration of this complex took place over the course of one hundred years.

Details on a lithograph of the interior of the San Fernando Church. An excellent piece, printed in the Church publication, La Cruz.

Convents for Friars

Exterior of the San Fernando College in 1855. The face of the clock installed in the church tower and, immediately to the left, an unusual little lantern that was added to all the school buildings, should be noted.

Exterior of San Fernando in 1857. Note the atrium wall, the tree filled atrium, the stone tiles and the gatekeeper's lodge on the left. The 1858 earthquake had not yet occurred, but the church had already sunk considerably into the city's swampy ground.

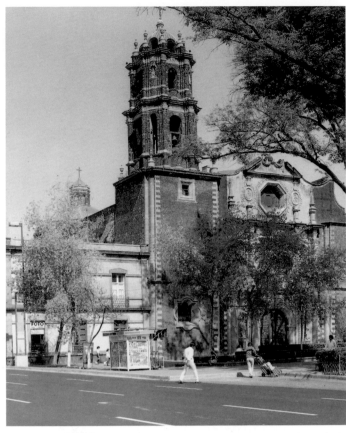

To the left, the exterior of the San Fernando Church in 1870. The stone ground and the trees in the atrium have disappeared, and the gatekeeper's lodge was demolished, as was the atrium wall. Almost one hundred years later, the square in front of San Fernando (on the right) was renovated, along with others in the city's Historic Center, in honor of the XIX Olympic games held in Mexico.

The modern day San Fernando Church. The destruction of the houses built up against its left hand side resulted in part of the convent being destroyed.

Above, the interior of the San Fernando Church in 1855. Full of gilded altarpieces, the extent of the devastation was such that only the pulpit was saved.
To the left, the same interior decorated in the Neoclassic style.

As in the case of San Francisco, the reproduction of an altarpiece similar to the original one, was possible thanks to an engraving from the last century.

The San Fernando College as seen from its church tower, depicted in an 1855 photograph.

Demolition of the remains of the San Fernando Convent and College in the nineteen thirties. These two photographs are very useful for the documentation of the history of barbarism in Mexico.

Santo Domingo Square around 1870. Leandro Valle Street, along the left side of the church, completed the separation of the Dominican Church and the convent. The latter was sold to private owners, thus beginning its degradation.

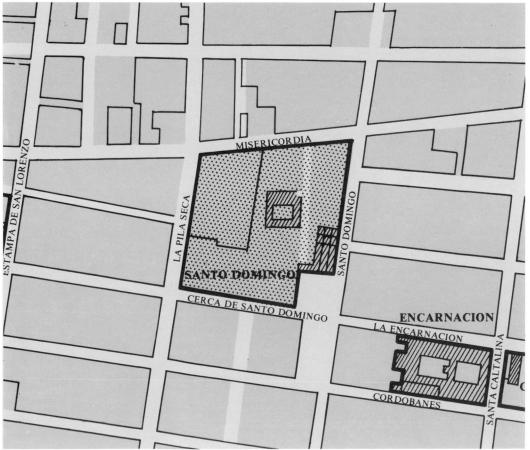

The location of the Santo Domingo Convent. The current street names are Republica de Chile (La Pila Seca), Republica de Peru (Misericordia) and Republica de Brazil (Santo Domingo). The name Cerca de Santo Domingo (today's Belisario Dominguez) referred to the atrium wall of the church, long since disappeared.

Imperial Santo Domingo de Mexico Convent

THE CONSTRUCTION of Santo Domingo de Mexico was begun in 1527. In 1550 however, both the church and the house were rebuilt; stone cutters Francisco Martin, Juan Sanchez Talaya and Gines Talaya took part in the construction. Claudio de Arciniega, Francisco Becerra and Juan de Alcantara (1557) took charge of the church. The latter was associated with the Dominican order, and the possibility exists that he may have participated in the construction of Yanhuitlan in Oaxaca. As for Becerra, we know that he took part in the building of the Dominican Church in Tepoztlan and that he traveled on to Peru after his stay in Mexico. During this period, the cloister was rebuilt because, according to the architects, the existing one was ruined. The new church, consecrated in 1590, was quite magnificent. It was described by chronicler Hernando de Ojea and we know that, around 1579, the sacristy was decorated with works by Pereyns, Requena and Zumaya. By 1790, the church had sunk and been flooded to such an extent that it was replaced by a new one, which was entrusted to Pedro de Arrieta.

The old convent grew, and during the XVII century it was transformed, its chapels were gradually opened. The Rosario Chapel, contemporary to and as ornate as the one in Puebla, was the work of Cristobal de Medina Vargas. It had altarpieces by Manuel de Velazco and was adorned with as much silver as the confraternity that supported it, possessed. In the XVIII century, it was endowed with Churrigueresque altarpieces by Isidoro Vicente de Balbas (1745). The Tercer Orden Chapel was decorated with altarpieces by Esquivel and Tomas Juarez, and in the XVIII century, it was redone by Lorenzo Rodriguez (1758) and adorned with Anaya altarpieces. The main church was extremely ornate, and a large part of it still remains. Nevertheless, the current situation of the convent is quite desolate. It is still invaded by courtyards of small, low income housing, and the possibility of saving what has survived seems quite remote. The fact is that in the case of Santo Domingo de Mexico, there is still a chance of adequately preserving its remains, if the necessary effort is made.

The major destruction of the convent began in April, 1861. The atrium wall was demolished, as were the arched gallery in the gatekeeper's lodge, the Tercer Orden Chapel and the Rosario Chapel, all to make way for a stupid street: Leandro Valle Street, which as Toussaint says, goes and comes from nowhere. We recommend reading Enrique Berlin's excellent work on the Santo Domingo Convent. The study by Ignacio Orejel and Manuel Gonzalez Beascoechea is also very useful, as are the documents on the church and convent published by Marco Dorta.

Convents for Friars

An extremely interesting photograph, previously unpublished, which allows us to enjoy the view of this church and convent while still intact. The odd relief, adorned on the lower part with a lambrequin, located on the wall separating the arches of the gatekeeper's lodge and the base of the tower, should be noted.

This superb photograph by Julio Michaud (c.1855), shows us the Dominican complex in the years prior to its destruction. The atrium wall and the two entablatured entrance doors, adorned with a broken pediment and the Dominican coat-of-arms, can be appreciated in full detail. The top floor of the arcade which led to the convent, and as in the case of San Francisco, was used as a library, can be seen. The cupola of the Tercer Orden Chapel, by Lorenzo Rodriguez, is also clearly visible and immediately behind the tower, the dome of the Rosario Chapel, which was rebuilt at the end of the XVIII century.

Convents for Friars

An 1863 photograph depicting the Dominican complex after the pickax's first wave of destruction. The atrium wall, the arcade of the gatekeeper's lodge and the sitting room of the old library have all disappeared. The Rosario Chapel was still standing because Leandro Valle Street had not yet been laid .

Above, an Iriarte lithograph showing Santo Domingo in May, 1861. The photograph on the right shows how the gatekeeper's lodge was rebuilt to close off the view of Leandro Valle Street. The work was done as part of the restoration process that was carried out for the XIX Olympic Games.

Convents for Friars

Above, the opening of Leandro Valle Street between April and May, 1861. Iriarte lithograph. To the left, a current view of the same street.

The Rosario Chapel transformed in Neoclassic style (Iriarte lithograph). The chapel no longer exists.

Convents for Friars

The old cloister of Santo Domingo. The convent had two other cloisters, of which only a few vestiges remain, since they were fully exploited as overcrowded, unhealthy tenements.

This tenement, one of the properties which resulted from the division of the Santo Domingo Convent, remains uninhabited after its evacuation following the 1985 earthquakes. In the background, the convent church.

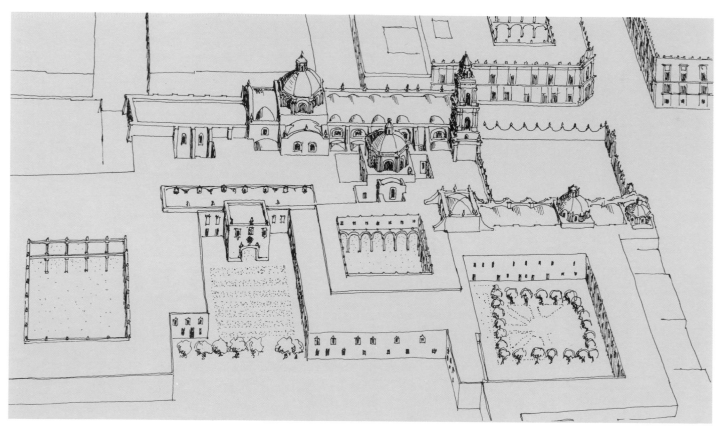

A hypothetical reconstruction of the Santo Domingo Convent based on a plan made in 1872, for the purpose of selling the building to private owners. To the right, we can see the Santo Domingo Square, which stretched the full length of the church.

Convents for Friars

The facade of the Tercer Orden Chapel. Note in the lower left hand corner, the foundation of the facade which was placed in front of the building, thus taking away its ecclesiastical air.

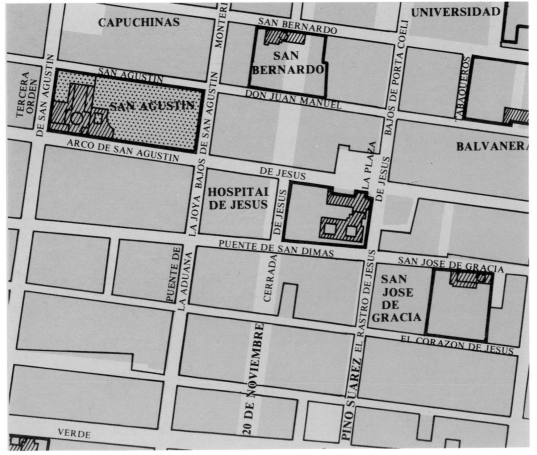

The location of the San Agustin Convent. None of the streets that bore the convent's name exist any longer. Los Bajos Street is now part of 5 de Febrero Street, Del Arco Street has merged into Republica de El Salvador and La Tercera Orden has become a section of Isabel la Catolica. The name Republica de Uruguay replaces that of San Agustin.

San Agustin Convent

THE CORNERSTONE of the Mexico City San Agustin Church was laid on August 28, 1541, by Viceroy Antonio de Mendoza. The church and convent were both quite lavish; the architect was Claudio de Arciniega, who around 1579, described the frontispiece of the church as adorned by "a great history of San Agustin...". The church was completed in 1587, and its main altarpiece was the work of Andres de la Concha; the wooden doors at the entrance were carved in 1591 by Pedro Lopez Pinto and Hernan Sanchez. This church was covered in carved wood that "was richly adorned with caissons and crossings and intertwinings with particular skill".

On Friday, December 11, 1676, at seven in the evening, the church and part of the convent caught fire. The roofing was consumed by the flames, and the blaze lasted for more than three days. Some of the lateral pieces and paintings were saved - among others, *Santa Cecilia*, by de la Concha, currently in the Viceregal Pinacotheca - and thanks to Don Juan de Chavarria, the magnificent Tabernacle was saved. Today, this heroic deed is remembered in a half-relief that decorates his house on today's Justo Sierra Street.

The reconstruction of the church was begun quickly. Brother Diego de Valverde, master architect; Tomas Juarez, sculptor, assembler and creator of the main altarpiece; Simon de Espinoza, gilder and Salvador de Ocampo, designer of the choir stalls, which had been miraculously saved and are preserved in the "Generalito" in San Ildefonso, all participated in the work. Architect Diego Rodriguez carried out several works in the convent at the end of the XVII century. In 1708, Jose Antonio de la Cruz built the now destroyed wall that surrounded the atrium. The church was decorated with altarpieces by Blas de los Angeles, Miguel Jose de Rivera, Juan de Rojas and Jose Joaquin de Sayago, who, in 1752, designed the main lateral piece of the Tercer Orden Chapel.

San Agustin was converted into the National Library, and the convent became a garbage heap, until it was completely destroyed. The beautiful cloister was damaged and what little remains of it is due to a miracle, since the rest, including several of the convent's buildings, were replaced by a parking lot.

Convents for Friars

Rear view of the San Agustin Convent during the mid XIX century. This interesting drawing gives us an idea of the magnitude of the capital's Augustine complex.

The exterior of San Agustin as depicted in an 1853 watercolor. The overall outer appearance of this magnificent building can be appreciated, at a time when the atrium wall still stood, and the church was still adorned with two towers. The three frontispieces are visible: the main one, adorned with a beautiful stone relief depicting San Agustin; the lateral facade, with a relief of the Virgin of Guadalupe and that of the Tercer Orden Chapel. All three were modified by Vicente de Heredia, who transformed the complex.

Above, the exterior of the same building after 1884. This photograph shows the conversion of the old church into a library. The Solomonic columns were saved, as was the relief on the main facade, although the abacus on the lateral facade disappeared. The facade of the Tercer Orden Chapel was kept in its original state, until it was finally concealed by another one, created to give uniformity to the new outer appearance.

To the right, a view of San Agustín after the conclusion of its exterior transformation.

Convents for Friars

The interior of San Agustin in 1855, as shown in a La Cruz lithograph. The church's magnificent appearance can be admired, with its wrought iron balustrades adorning the windows above the chapels in the nave, its old wooden pulpit and elegant main altarpiece, which was the work of the chief sculptor from Chimalhuacan Atenco. The altarpiece came close to being destroyed by fire in 1574, but was rescued, only to be reduced to firewood in 1861.

Above, the interior of San Agustin in 1884. Compare this with the previous illustration, and note how the church was modified when it was converted into the National Library. This was a rather foolish use if we consider the lack of light and, above all, the cold interior, as mentioned by Manuel Romero de Terreros, in his study on this building.

To the right, a present day view. The wall relief is no more than a mural of the Tercer Orden frontispiece, which was next to the church. The frontispiece is almost completely intact, although it has been hidden by the new facade.

A view of the main cloister of San Agustin. This is all that remained of the magnificent Renaissance courtyard. Part of it was saved, and the rest, turned into a parking lot.

*Above, a panoramic **view** of the Augustinian Convent. The bell tower of the San Agustin Church was one of the highest in the city. From this spot, the renowned Italian artist, Pedro Gualdi, created this and other lithographs, several of which have been included to illustrate this book.*

To the right, a current view of the cloister. It was very common for the Augustinians to build more arches on the second floor than on the first. Due to this peculiarity, it is a shame that only a small part of the courtyard still exists.

Convents for Friars

La Merced Church with its truly outstanding roofing, the negligent loss of which, must be included among the more painful ones we have found out about. The bell tower on the left belongs to the Mercedarios Church; the one on the right, slightly more in the foreground, belongs to the Balvanera Chapel.

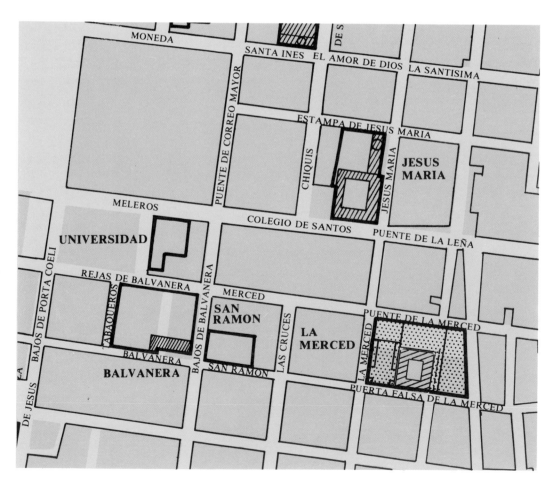

The three streets which formerly bore the convent's name, have since been lost. Puente Street is now Garcia Bravo Square, which was created at the expense of the convent. La Estampa Street is now part of Jesus Maria Street, and La Puerta Falsa Street has become part of Republica de Uruguay Street. A section of the current Talavera Street passed through the convent.

Nuestra Señora de las Mercedes Convent, Redemption of the Imprisoned

ALTHOUGH BROTHER BARTOLOME DE OLMEDO, a member of the order of la Merced, was the first to set foot on Mexican soil, the members of this order did not settle in the Kingdom of New Spain until the last quarter of the XVI century. By 1593, they had completed a small convent in Mexico City, located in the San Lazaro Neighborhood. Around 1601, they purchased the houses of Guillermo Borondate and decided to build a church, the first stone of which was laid on September 8, 1602. This building, repaired over time, was the Tercer Orden Chapel, until it was torn down in 1861. In 1634, the decision to construct a new building was made, which was virtually finished in 1654.

Architect Lazaro de Torres was involved in the work on the church and convent. Although the dates on the documents that we have studied are somewhat distant-the first mention of him was in 1634-in 1679, the architect appeared before chronicler Baltazar Morante, and we assume that we are dealing with the same person. On October 30, 1679, the members of the La Merced order decided to gather one hundred neighbors together, in order to make them into patrons of the church and convent. On July 6, 1680, they all came before the notary and witnesses, among them, Captain Juan de Vera, who arranged for his and his family's burial in the church that was soon to be built. The chapels were also built and embellished. Los Morenos, for example, was decorated with altarpieces by Tomas Juarez, and the San Jose Chapel was opened in 1683. In 1693, the patrons of the church assembled once again, and a collection was organized to build the tower and cloister. In 1695, Blas de la Santa Maria was engaged to create the main altarpiece of the church.

According to chronicler Antonio de Robles, the cloister was opened in 1703, and the church was also finished around the same time. The new main altarpiece, adorned with balustered columns, was made in 1737, and in 1742, Francisco Antonio de Anaya began working on the lateral pieces for the nave.

Disaster began to strike this convent in 1861. Julio Lavarrier provides an excellent description, written the same year, of how the library was looted and the church, roofed with the last great caissioned ceiling in the city, was destroyed. The convent archives were burnt.

Convents for Friars

Exterior of la Merced Church in 1853. Thanks to this watercolor, we can get an idea of what La Merced looked like, with its atrium wall, gatekeeper's lodge, church with three entrances, magnificent tower and unique, caissoned ceilings. It was barbarically demolished.

Interior of La Merced Church in 1855. In keeping with the Neoclassic style, the friars had already substituted the gilded main altarpiece. However, the lateral pieces located at the back of the right processional nave are original. The same applies to the pulpit. The Mudejar ceiling and several stalls can also be seen. All of this disappeared in 1861. Lithograph by Decaen.

The spot where La Merced Church once stood is now a vacant lot. The only reminders of this magnificent church are the arches on the left hand side, and the pilasters embedded in the wall enclosing the property.

Convents for Friars

View of La Merced Church from the cloister. This cloister, finished in 1703, was adorned with paintings that have all disappeared. The church's odd, conically-shaped, spire-like cupola can be seen. The lithograph is by Gualdi.

Cloister of La Merced in 1855. We can appreciate the wrought iron banister and the old well, covered by a roof supported by four columns.

To the right, La Merced cloister. When the complex was disentailed, this cloister was turned into a barracks, and many additions made it completely unrecognizable. Miraculously enough, it was not demolished. In 1915, Doctor Atl approached Venustiano Carranza to try and save this marvelous building, and it should be recognized that thanks to the efforts of artist and art historian, the building is in decent condition today.

In the photograph below, we can appreciate the wrought iron banisters and other of the cloister's architectural elements, which were brought here after being salvaged from other viceregal buildings that have since disappeared.

Convents for Friars

During the mid XX century, the main Montserrat cloister was used for housing. It was then decided to widen Izazaga Street, with the consequences shown in this photograph. What survived the broadening of the street is now the Charreria Museum.

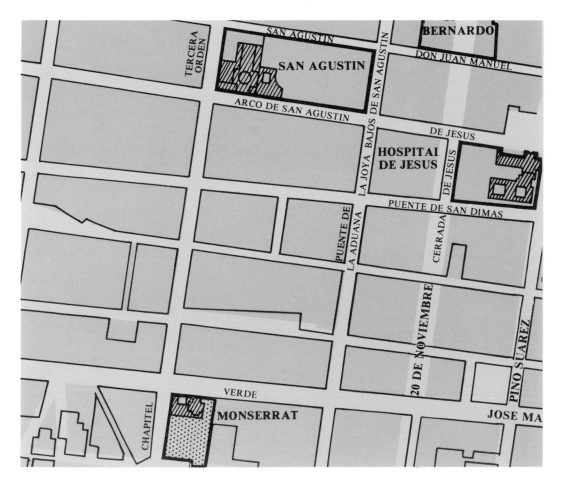

Location of the Montserrat Convent. Verde Street is now called Izazaga, and Chapitel de Montserrat Street is Isabel la Catolica.

Our Lady of Montserrat

IN NEW SPAIN, THE BENEDICTINE FRIARS, one of the richest and most powerful orders in Europe, had little more than a small house on the edge of Mexico City. Upon their arrival in 1614, Brothers Diego Sanchez and Juan Vitoria were given a chapel named after the Virgin of Monte Serrato, and which at the time, had been closed. The Benedictine friars built their monastery around this chapel, upon which they also made some improvements. The foundation never attained the dimensions of the large mendicant convents, but it did have an abundant library and valuable paintings, among which was one attributed to Zurbaran.

The loss of the Benedictine estate began a short time before Independence, when in January 1821, the closure of the monastery was decreed. Under the new Reform Laws the building was divided into plots, thus accelerating its destruction, and by the mid XXth century, its main cloister had become housing units. It was then decided to widen Izazaga Street, the consequences of which are shown in the photographs. The Charreria Museum is housed today in the section that survived the broadening of the street.

Monserrat at the time when the convent and the church were torn down. Fortunately, part of the complex was saved.

79

Convents for Friars

La Profesa Cloister during its demolition in 1861. It was once adorned with canvases by Cabrera and panels by Echave and other masters. This was a typical example of Jesuit architecture, as shown by its high, enclosed cloister. Nothing remains of this building.

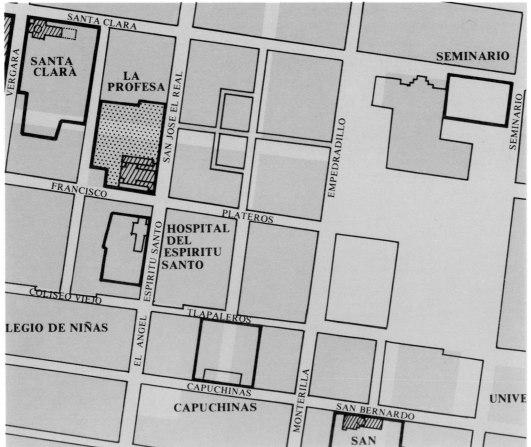

Location of La Profesa House. The corner of San Jose el Real and San Francisco streets is now known as Isabel la Catolica and Madero streets. In some maps, this section of San Francisco Street was called Plateros and even La Profesa Street.

La Casa Profesa of the Society of Jesus

THE OLD JESUIT CASA PROFESA DE EJERCICIOS was a noteworthy complex that consisted of a church and an enormous annex. The old construction was begun in the XVI century and disappeared during the XVIII century. The primitive church had an altarpiece by Baltazar de Echave Orio that was later replaced by one created by Juan de Rojas in 1699. It had a Mudejar-style wooden cover of which some fragments remain in the choir stalls of the current church, which are the work of Pedro de Arrieta. Although it is still in existence, this magnificent church lost its lofty gilded altarpieces when they were replaced by Neoclassic ones by Manuel Tolsa. As we can gather from the comments made by Couto in his *Dialogue on Painting in Mexico,* and the rich harvest that he obtained from the members of the Oratory order - who took over La Profesa when the Jesuits were expelled - the building's Pinacotheca was extremely rich and made important contributions to the San Carlos collection with works such as, *Santos Justo y Pastor,* by Jose Juarez and *San Alejo,* - painted by the same artist - which arrived unharmed but, due to unforgivable carelessness a few years ago, was turned into a colorless rag. It is now being restored thanks to the efforts of Mercedes Meade and Virginia Armella de Aspe, who are responsible for the Viceregal Pinacotheca of San Diego. As we have repeatedly stated in this book - its collection was made up of the paintings from the now extinct convents of Mexico's capital city.

It must be pointed out that a notable collection of paintings, furniture and sculptures is still kept in La Profesa. Works by Pedro de Mena, the sculptor from Granada, can be seen in the sacristy of the church, as well as a magnificent piece of furniture that is believed to have come from the San Agustin Convent. The collection of paintings is considerable and, among its main artistic exponents, are Villalpando, Echave and Cabrera.

IX Convents for Nuns

DURING THE VICEREGAL ERA, twenty convents for nuns were built in Mexico City. These buildings belonged to Conceptionists (La Concepcion, Regina, Jesus Maria, La Encarnacion, Santa Ines, Balvanera, San Jose de Gracia and San Bernardo), Franciscans (Santa Clara, San Juan de la Penitencia, Santa Isabel, Capuchinas and Corpus Christi), Augustinians (San Lorenzo), Dominicans (Santa Catalina de Siena), Carmelites (Santa Teresa la Antigua and la Nueva), Order of the Saviour (Santa Brigida) and the Society of Mary (La Enseñanza Antigua and Nueva).

To date, no historic-artistic study of the architectural typography of the convents for nuns has been done. There are essays on their history (Josefina Muriel) and on particular details of their architecture, as in the case of the positioning of choirs within their churches. Perhaps this is due to the absence of any complexes still intact, and above all, to the lack of plans that could give us an idea of what they were like. Nevertheless, archive research could provide us with some findings like those presented further on, for example: the plans of Balvanera, Santa Clara and Santa Isabel, drawn up to facilitate the division of the buildings into tracts sold to private buyers in 1861. In these plans, we perceived the complex structure of the buildings, which consisted of a large number of small spaces whose function is as of yet unknown to us, although it can be deduced through study and common sense. One XVIII century plan of the Jesus Maria Convent does exist, published by Josefina Muriel, which contains ample indications as to the function of its spaces, but it is an exceptional case.

Of the twenty convents for nuns in Mexico City, the Regina, Jesus Maria, Santa Ines, La Encarnacion and La Enseñanza convents are all almost intact, although they did not escape Neoclassicism, secularization and all kinds of modifications. La Concepcion, Santa Catalina de Siena and Santa Teresa la Antigua have preserved their churches and parts of their convents. Balvanera, San Jose de Gracia, Santa Clara, Corpus Christi, San Lorenzo and Santa Teresa la Nueva have only conserved their churches. In no case do altarpieces or other artistic treasures remain and, in the cases of San Juan de la Penitencia, Capuchinas, Santa Isabel, Santa Brigida and La Enseñanza Nueva (the latter was transitory, as it was established on one side of Loreto, nothing is left of it and its nuns ended up in Betlemitas), nothing more than information, a few photographs and the memory of these exists. In the case

of San Bernardo, half of the church is still standing. It could thus be said that they had the same, if not worse fate, as the convents for friars.

The destruction of these buildings which took place between 1861 and 1940, is one of the saddest chapters in the history of the destruction of monuments in Mexico City. Their much acclaimed wealth included magnificent buildings, paintings, sculptures, ivories, jewelry, gold and silver pieces and libraries. When they were seized, no inventories were taken; and so we do not even know what was lost or what became of these possessions. A few chronicles give us an idea of what existed.

The oldest, largest and richest convent was La Concepcion. In 1861, it owned 127 pieces of property in Mexico City. La Encarnacion owned 82 pieces of land and San Jeronimo 92. With the nationalization of these properties, all this was liquidated in an instant, much to the benefit of a group of land owners and urban property speculators. It was unlikely that one thousand properties would end up providing income for five hundred women dedicated to a religious life, who had the following activities: La Concepcion, flowers and pastries; Regina, cleansing powders and eye drops;

The upper choir of Santa Catalina, seen from the same angle as the nuns when they attended mass.

84

Jesus Maria, sweets; San Jeronimo, candied pumpkin; Balvanera, artificial flowers; La Encarnacion, flavored beverages and pink honey; San Lorenzo, sugar paste and candies; Santa Brigida, ruffles; La Enseñanza Antigua, weavings and embroideries, and La Enseñanza Nueva, chocolate and prepared food.

The nuns had maids and, in the XVII century, the wealthiest lived in small houses throughout the cloisters and other spaces. With the famous exception of Sor Juana, they were not concerned with cultural matters. There were theologian nuns like Maria Ana Agueda de San Ignacio, but most of them made embroideries, reliquaries and artistic curios. There was a whole artistic genre, which has practically disappeared, that consisted of making miniature objects as toys, and puerile attempts at reducing the world to fit into their own scope; I have seen Nativity scenes and scenes of Saint Pascual Bailon in his kitchen, that remind me of doll houses.

The churches generally had twin portals, and the choirs were integrated into the church in such a way, that the nuns attended mass behind a gate. The convents had domestic chapels and typically, locutories and revolving reception windows at the entrances. Nuns spent their lives in such silence and peace -although there were disagreements during the abbess elections- that at the time of the religious persecutions, the Santa Monica Convent had to be discovered by air by the famous detective Valente Quintana. Such was the secrecy within which they lived. Nowadays, the Carmelites probably have portraits of the founders of their order and of several of the nuns that professed the faith in Santa Teresa la Antigua. Others have kept papers and books, but these are insignificant when compared to what they had until the middle of the XIX century.As we shall duly explain, almost all of the famous artists in Mexico City worked for the churches and convents of nuns. Regina and La Enseñanza were the only churches that were saved from Neoclassicism, even though in the former, the *Nuestra Señora de las Tres Necesidades* altarpiece was destroyed. All of the other convents lost their Baroque heritage, because of secularization and disentailment, or due to the nuns' own initiative. Destruction has not been the private sport of a single group, but the pastime of almost all Mexicans.

Interior chapel of La Concepcion Convent, with its Churrigueresque door. It was demolished. Photograph from around 1861.

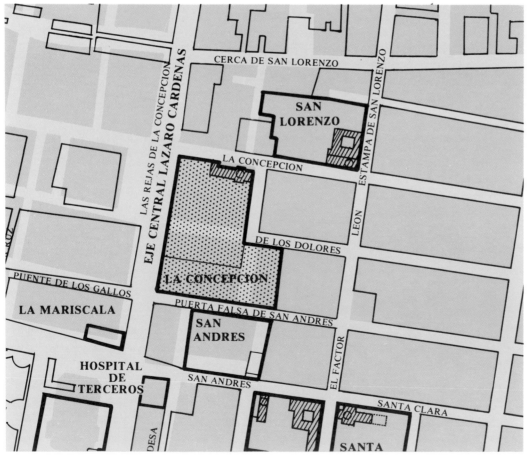

Location of La Concepcion Convent. The street that bore the convent's name is now called Belisario Dominguez. Puerta Falsa de San Andres Street adopted the name Donceles. The Los Dolores Alley was extended and is now called Republica de Cuba. 57 Street was laid by crossing the convent from north to south.

La Concepción

THE OLDEST, LARGEST AND MOST DAMAGED monastery for nuns was La Concepcion. It deserves an ample and meticulous monograph because it was the prototype for all the others. Its church, with its caissoned ceiling and altarpiece by Pedro de Requena and Juan Gomez (1580), was already important during the XVI century. The current church, dating from around 1655, had altarpieces by Nicolas de Vergara (1664) and Juan de Rojas (1704). Nevertheless, the most important was the main one created by Jeronimo de Balbas in 1748, of which only the documents in the Notary Archives and General Archives of the Nation remain. This was one of the most important Churrigueresque altarpieces in New Spain. It was reduced to firewood, in order to make way for a graceless Neoclassic one. The tutelary image is magnificent: I am referring to the XVII century *Purisima Concepcion* that still exists, and is carved in wood, with "Estofado" decorations. The convent, a true citadel, was divided up into lots and ruined. Only a few remnants of it remain.

Pool and cell in another of La Concepcion Cloisters, around 1861.

Convents for Nuns

One of the cloisters of La Concepcion in 1861. Images can still be seen on the wall dating from the year the place was passed on to its new inhabitants, who are shown in this photograph. After serving as a tenement, it was demolished.

This photograph shows us the same cloister, exactly as it looked during the nineteen thirties.

Top floor of La Concepcion Cloister. In the following photograph, this gallery appears in the background. It should be pointed out that this cloister retained its original layout in 1861. In other words, the cells, chapel and pool contained within its area, and only two of its sides had a gallery of columns, without arches.

Demolition of one cloister and various cells at La Concepcion 1862.

Detail of the mural painting in the Jesus Maria Cloister.

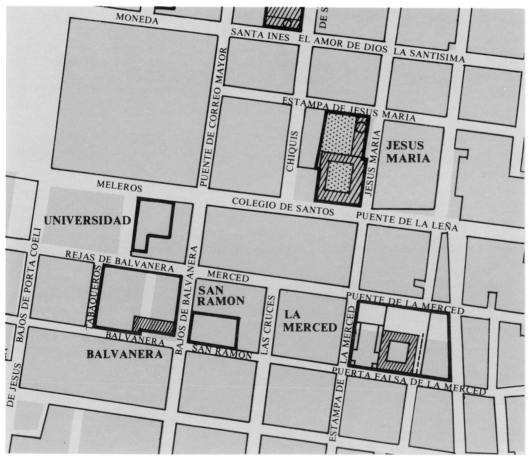

Location of the Jesus Maria Convent. Only Jesus Maria Street still has its original name. Colegio de Santos Street is now Corregidora, and Estampa de Jesus Maria Street now bears the name of La Soledad.

The Royal Monastery
of Jesus Maria

THANKS TO CARLOS DE SIGUENZA Y GONGORA, the author of a chronicle relating all sorts of details, the story of this building is very well known. Entitled *Western Paradise*, it is of enormous interest because, aside from including the history of the monastery, it has terrible, but very amusing biographies of the nuns. The monastery was founded for the daughters of Conquistadors and impoverished Spaniards. One of King Felipe II's daughters and the sister of Inquisitor, Archbishop and Viceroy of New Spain, Don Pedro Moya de Contreras, came to this convent.

We know of one XVIII century plan of the convent that, along with the description given by Siguenza and some of the documents on such artists as Luis Juarez and Pedro Ramirez who participated in the project, give us an idea of the splendor of this complex. At the end of the XVIII century, Jose Antonio Gonzalez Velazquez transformed the church in the Neoclassic style.

From 1861 onwards, the convent was used for a variety of purposes moviehouse, billiards hall, tenement- and during this century, the church was used as the Archives of the Ministry of Defense. Despite the fact that it now houses a furniture and home appliance store, this complex is perhaps one of the most complete convents of nuns still in existence.

Plan of the convent, taken from a photograph from the old Colonial Monument Archives. XVIII century.

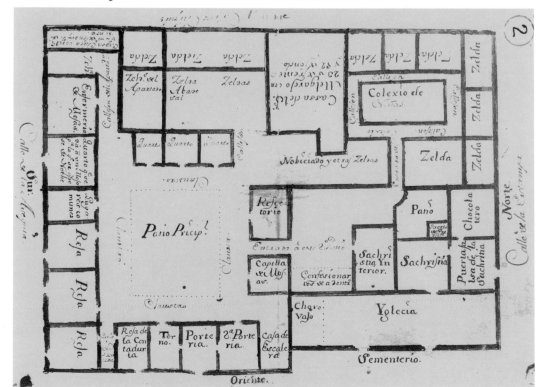

On the left, the cloister of the Jesus Maria Convent (c.1860). Below. View of one of the corridors that led to several of the cells in the Jesus Maria Convent (c. 1861).

Arches of the Jesus Maria Cloister. On the back wall, XVIII century mural paintings with Guadalupan scenes can be admired (c.1860).

The Jesus Maria Cloister as an electrical appliance shop. Among its other uses, it was a movie house, at which time it was roofed. It still retains some of the fantasy-like decor and modifications made when it served this purpose.

La Encarnacion Cloister in 1860. The fountain and garden were still intact.

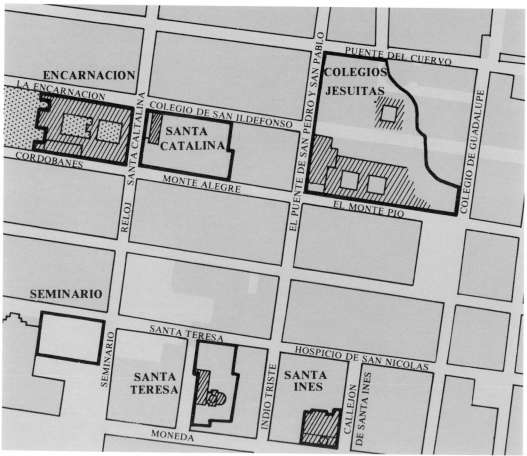

Location of La Encarnacion Convent. Encarnacion Street is now Republica de Venezuela and its parallel street, Cordobanes, is now Luis Gonzalez Obregon. Santa Catalina Street is today Republica de Argentina.

La Encarnacion

FOUNDED IN 1594, La Encarnacion Monastery has undergone countless transformations. For example, its church which was consecrated in 1648, once had coffered wood that no longer exists. Its XVII century altarpieces were the work of Manuel de Velazco and Juan de Rojas, and its organs were made by Tiburcio Saenz de Izaguirre and Jose Casela (1746). Its exuberance was noteworthy; Marchioness Calderon de la Barca gives a detailed description of it in her book *Life in Mexico*. After 1861, it was used as a storehouse for the paintings taken by the government from the secularized convents. Fortunately, Manuel Constanso's marvelous cloister is still in existence, since Jose Vasconcelos had the foresight to conserve and expand it and offer its walls to Diego Rivera and other important muralists.

On the left, La Encarnacion Cloister. Its builder, Manuel Constanso, was one of the most talented exponents of Neoclassicism in New Spain. On the right, one of the corridors in La Encarnacion, which are now decorated with Diego Rivera murals.

Demolition of the Santa Ines Tower in March, 1861.

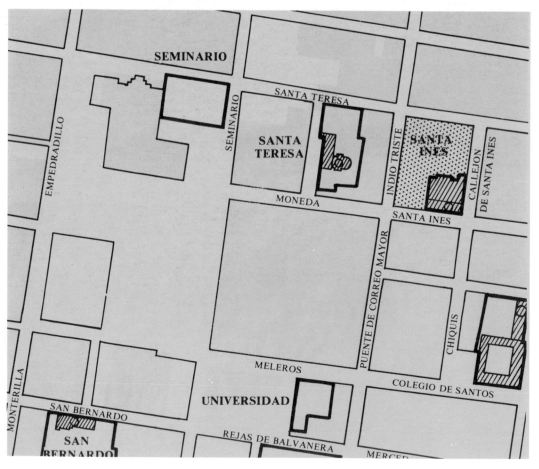

Location of the Santa Ines Convent. Santa Ines Alley is now called Academia, and the name Moneda was extended east, substituting that of Santa Ines.

Santa Ines

THE OLD CONSTRUCTION DISAPPEARED at the end of the XVIII century. In 1790, work was done on the church that we know nowadays. Rather than renovated, it was rebuilt by Francisco de Guerrero y Torres.

The church was dismantled in 1861 and became a fodder warehouse. The very high, slim, beautiful tower was demolished. The cloister is still preserved.

The Santa Ines Cloister as it was during the secularization period. On the right, a present day photograph.

Convents for Nuns

The Balvanera Cloister in 1861.

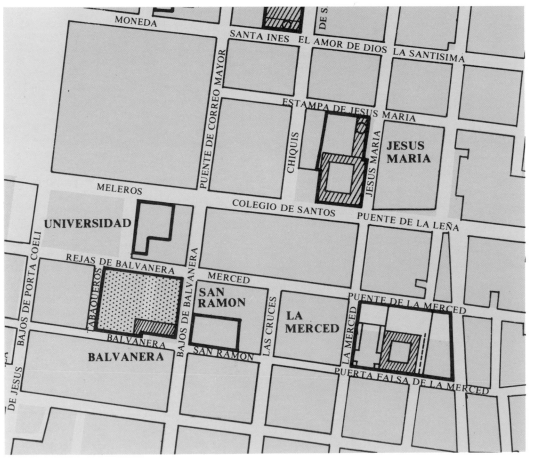

Location of the Balvanera Convent. The three streets that bore the name Balvanera have long since discarded it. Las Rejas became Venustiano Carranza, Los Bajos is now Correo Mayor and the third is Republica de Uruguay. Only Tabaqueros Alley remains, the alley that cut across the convent is called Yucatan.

Balvanera

FORMERLY CALLED JESUS DE LA PENITENCIA, its patron, doña Beatriz de Miranda paid for its construction. The church was opened in 1671. During the same year, Manuel de Velazco created the altarpieces for the interior of the church, and glassworker Mateo de Chavez made the windows. In 1749, Francisco Martinez created the new main lateral piece of balustered columns, which was destroyed by the Neoclassical designs during the XIX century. The convent was very large and in 1861, was sold as lots, until it completely disappeared during the present century.

Rear courtyard of the Balvanera Convent in 1860.

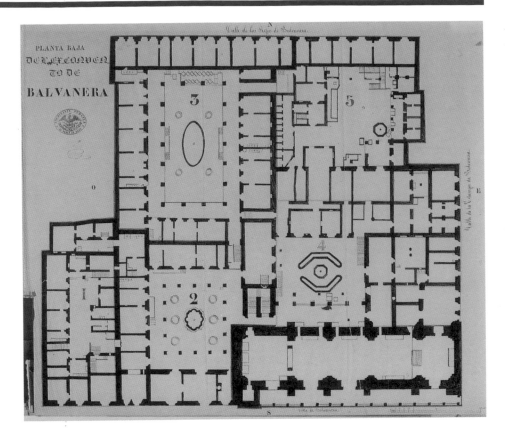

Plan of the Balvanera Convent. Below, the cloister during its demolition in the nineteen thirties. The shape of the columns shows us that it is the same building as in the photograph on the previous page.

Plan of the Balvanera Convent. Below, a hypothetical reconstruction of the convent, based on these plans from the Notary Archives.

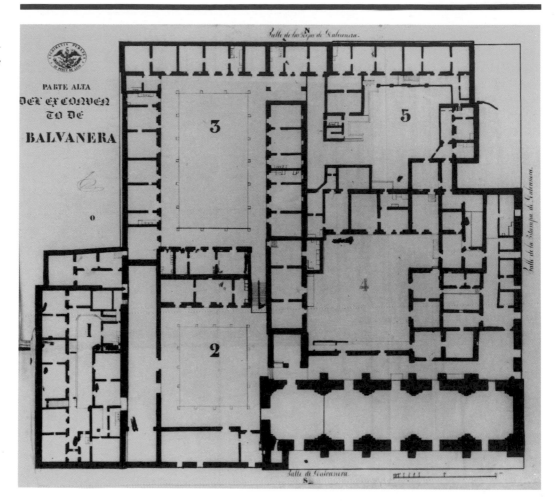

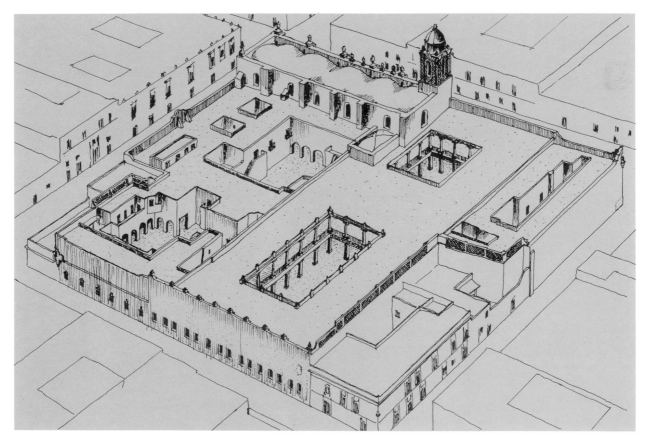

Convents for Nuns

The cupola of the San Jose de Gracia Church allows us to identify this photograph.

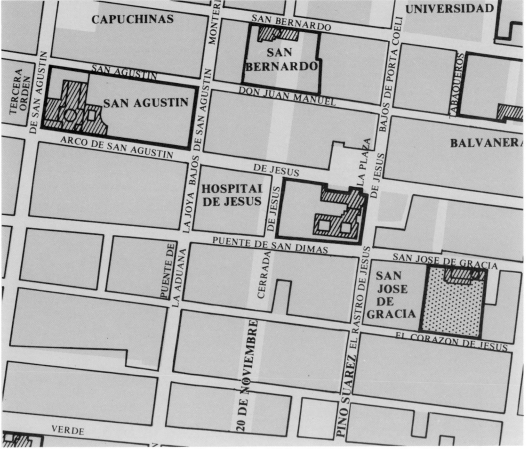

Location of the San Jose de Gracia Convent. San Jose de Gracia Street now bears the name of Mesones, one of the few surviving from Viceregal times. Corazon de Jesus Street is now called Regina, and Rastro de Jesus is Pino Suarez

San Jose de Gracia

AROUND 1610, A RICH MAN FROM THE CITY, don Fernando de Villegas, went before Archbishop Brother Garcia Guerra and Viceroy Luis de Velazco, attempting to found a monastery for nuns, for which he had to go through a long and painstaking bureaucratic process. He achieved his goal, although the old building was very meagre. Thus around 1658, the nuns decided to improve their house and church, and for this purpose, they procured the help of don Juan Navarro Pastrana, who gave them the money. On March 6, 1659, the trust was established before an actuary, and the church was consecrated in 1661. In 1664, Antonio Maldonado created an altarpiece, and Diego de Velazco made another in 1668. Naturally, they no longer exist. The church, which was looted, remains, although the convent was demolished in the nineteen fifties, to allow a disgusting building to be built in its place.

A corridor in the convent's cloister.

Convents for Nuns

Above, the side of the church as seen from the school yard which now stands in the place of the convent. Other buildings that were part of the complex were lost when a building which no longer exists was built. The 1985 earthquakes hastened their demise, though not so for the church.

On the left, the San Jose de Gracia Cloister in the hands of the army, because before its destruction, it was a barracks.

On the right, the same convent, around 1926. The supports on the upper cloister are proof that both negligence and the phantom of progress are the product of ignorance, and are active agents in the destruction of cultural heritage.

Reconstruction of one of the frontispieces near 20 de Noviembre (1938).

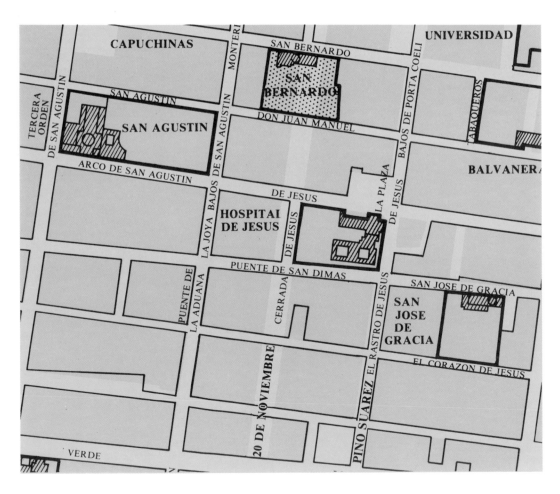

Location of the San Bernardo Convent. The street named for the convent is now part of Venustiano Carranza. Don Juan Manuel Street is now Republica de Uruguay.

San Bernardo

AROUND 1653, the rivalries among the Conceptionist nuns of the Regina Convent resulted in the founding of the San Bernardo Convent. However, as of 1621, a commitment was undertaken to found a convent for the Cistercian Order, with the financial backing of merchant Juan Marquez de Orozco. The buildings that existed prior to the patronage of Captain Juan de Retes y Lagarche were extremely poor.

On June 24, 1685, the cornerstone was laid, and the church was consecrated in 1690. During this period, the following artists participated in different work: Diego Gonzalez, carpenter and author of works in San Pablo, made the wooden doors for the church around 1687. Pedro Maldonado created the main altarpiece in 1688 and a lateral piece with paintings by Cristobal de Villalpando in 1690. The frontispieces were sculpted by Nicolas de Covarrubias in 1689. Manuel de Velazco and his brother Antonio also made lateral pieces for the church. The organ built by Tiburcio Saenz de Izaguirre of Aragon was first played in 1709. In 1777, the church was renovated and lost its former decor, which was described in the fascinating book Holy Register, published in 1691. I reproduced this description in its entirety in the first volume of my *Bibliography of the Art of New Spain.*

The convent was demolished in 1861, but the church was only looted. Neoclassicism had already been at work, destroying the Churrigueresque altarpieces in 1777.

The exterior of the San Bernardo Church before it was transformed in order to make way for 20 de Noviembre Street (c. 1920).

Above, the exterior of San Bernardo during the demolition of half of the church.
On the right, a current shot.

The unique bell tower of Santa Clara.

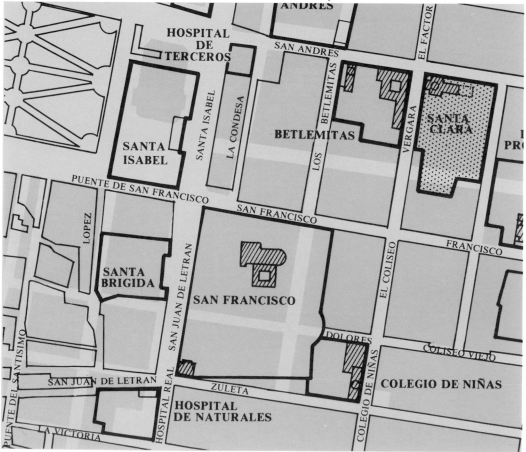

Location of the Santa Clara Convent. Vergara Street is now Bolivar which, to the north becomes Republica de Chile. The parallel street that runs east is now Motolinia, and Santa Clara is called Tacuba. The convent's name lives on as that of a large office block built on its land.

Santa Clara

THE MAGNIFICENT SANTA CLARA CONVENT, whose church was opened in 1661, acquired considerable importance in the XVIII century, especially after the 1755 fire, when all of its damage was repaired. It was totally destroyed in the XIX century. By 1867, nothing was left of the convent except the church and the Purisima Concepcion Chapel, which later became a liquor store. After being used as a barracks and even an observatory, it was sold to Mr. Hagenbeck, who tore it down. Fortunately, we located an 1861 plan that provides an approximate idea of the complex.

The convent's cloister in 1861. Lithograph by Iriarte.

The cloister of Santa Clara in 1860. This, as yet unpublished photograph, shows us the cloister's three floors in the eastern part of the building.

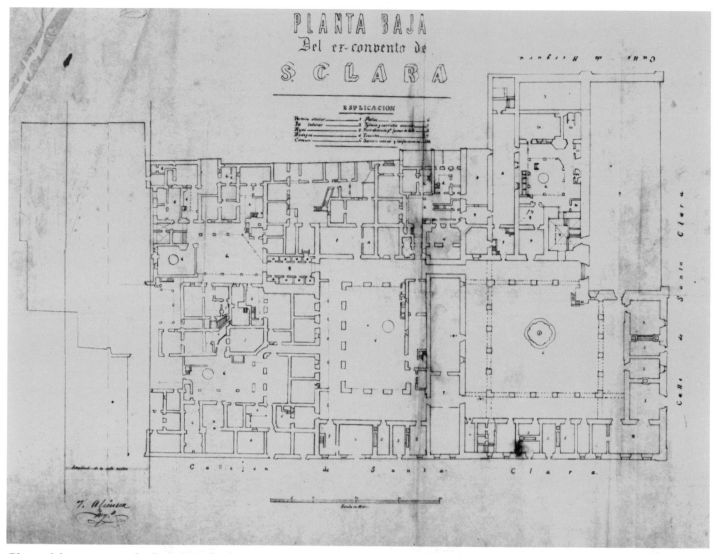

Plans of the convent and a hypothetical reconstruction based on the same document.

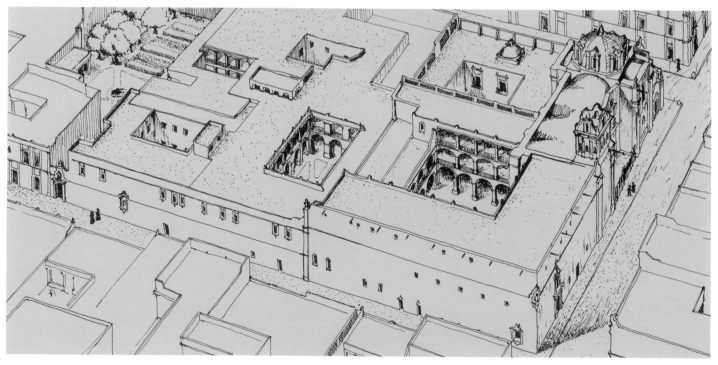

Convents for Nuns

View of the Santa Clara Convent as seen in a lithograph by Iriarte (1861). Note how the extremely original tower was formed by four bell gables, and how the building on the corner, which is none other than the Betlemitas Hospital, boasts a vaulted niche and richly decorated windows on the third floor. All of this has been lost.

This lithograph published by Manuel Rivera Cambas, shows how the degradation of the property began with the demolition of its belfry.

Modern day view of the same corner. The choirs and tower of this church were totally demolished. A subway station now occupies the spot.

Convents for Nuns

The San Juan de la Penitencia Bell Tower. The loss represented by the demolition of this tower is felt more profoundly, when compared to other church belfries in this book.

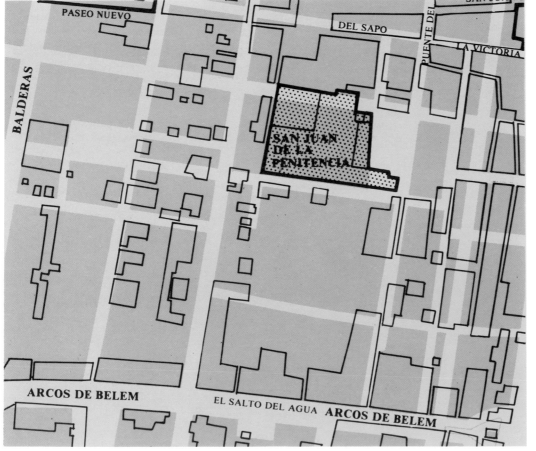

Location of the San Juan de la Penitencia Convent. The white area in front of the convent and the street that ran along its southern border, are now called Ernesto Pugibet Street. The convent's name survives, through the San Juan Market, which was built on convent land.

San Juan de la Penitencia

WHERE THE BUEN TONO CHURCH now stands, there was first a hermitage, then a hospice and lastly, a Clarist monastery and temple. The church, which lasted until the beginning of this century, was the second building to occupy the spot during the XVII century. Juan Salcedo de Espinoza worked on the church, which belonged to the hospice at the beginning of the XVII century. It is interesting that Juana Oliva de Villaseñor donated sixty thousand pesos for the second nuns' church, as was stated in the deed drawn up by Martin del Rio on September 16, 1694. The cornerstone for this new construction was laid in 1695, and it was opened in 1711. The altarpieces from this period were made by artists of the stature of Jacinto Nadal y Lluvet, a Catalonian assembler and gilder, a partner of Antonio Maldonado and altarpiece craftsman in Atlixco at the end of the XVII century.

The church was "renovated" in 1862. It is amazing that right in the midst of the secularization period, the nuns destroyed the altarpieces as well as the

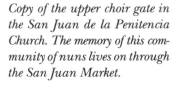

Copy of the upper choir gate in the San Juan de la Penitencia Church. The memory of this community of nuns lives on through the San Juan Market.

117

Exterior of the San Juan de la Penitencia Church. Demolished to make way for another church, it had two frontispieces that had no equal anywhere in the country. The photograph is from the beginning of the century.

On the opposite page, the interior of the San Juan de la Penitencia Church. The upper choir is still behind the gate, but the lower one, baldachin and all, was turned into a chapel.

Baroque decor; clearly, whatever the Reform did not achieve, the clergy did. The nuns' choir gate was an outstanding example of casting work from around 1862. When the church was demolished so that the Buen Tono Church could be erected, Doctor Aureliano Urrutia had the gate removed and took it to a hospital in Coyoacan. Later, it was moved to Chapultepec Castle. By some absurd arrangement, a copy was placed at the entrance to Chapultepec, where it can be admired from Reforma Avenue. It was placed between two bronze lions that were rescued from the Legislative Palace, the construction of which was interrupted by the outbreak of the Revolution.

Old Santa Isabel Street at the end of the XIX century. Note the use of the church as a silk factory and how its facade is hidden behind the houses that were built in its atrium. The beginning of the demolition of houses, to make way for the square of what was then known as the National Theater, can be seen.

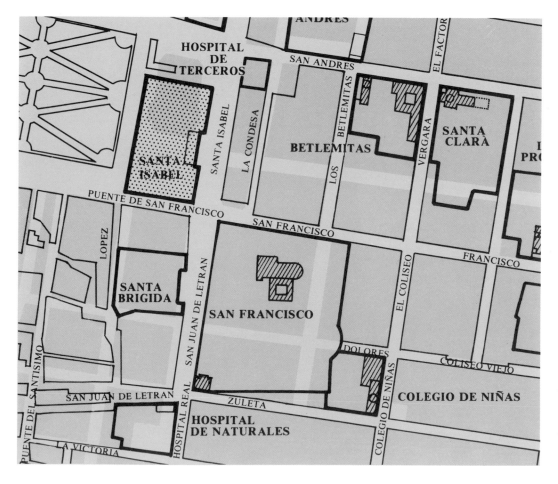

Location of the Santa Isabel Convent. The gray shaded area pinpoints the position of the Fine Arts Palace with respect to the convent. The old Puente de San Francisco Street is now the considerably wider Juarez Avenue.

Santa Isabel

IN 1600, THE NUNS OF SANTA CLARA decided to found another convent. They requested a papal bull and carried out all the necessary procedures. They got doña Catalina de Peralta to offer them her houses for the convent and obtained her personal commitment, as she was their first novice. When excavations for the foundation of the Fine Arts Palace were begun, the burial place of this woman was located, and when the body was uncovered -still clothed- the workers noticed that she was wearing jewelry. The only thing that remains is a tombstone, which was exhibited by the Architecture Division of the National Institute of Fine Arts, a short time ago.

In 1676 the church was rebuilt and was dedicated in 1681, this time under the patronage of Diego del Castillo, a very well known personage, as he was also the patron of the Dieguino Churubusco Convent. The figures of don Diego and his wife are exhibited in the museum that now stands in that spot. I have seen the convent's patronage in documents dated March 11, 1678 and signed before the actuary Pedro Vidal de Fuentes, on file in the Notary Archives. The interior of the church had altarpieces by Juan Montero and Manuel de Velazco. Jose Sagayo, the famous carpenter also made a lateral piece for the church, but none of these pieces survived. In the XVIII century it had an altarpiece by Isidoro Vicente de Balbas, and in 1852 they were all converted to the Neoclassic style. In 1861 the community was secularized, and the church was turned into a warehouse and later a factory. The convent was divided into plots. At the end of the XIX century it was completely demolished, and the Fine Arts Palace was built in its place.

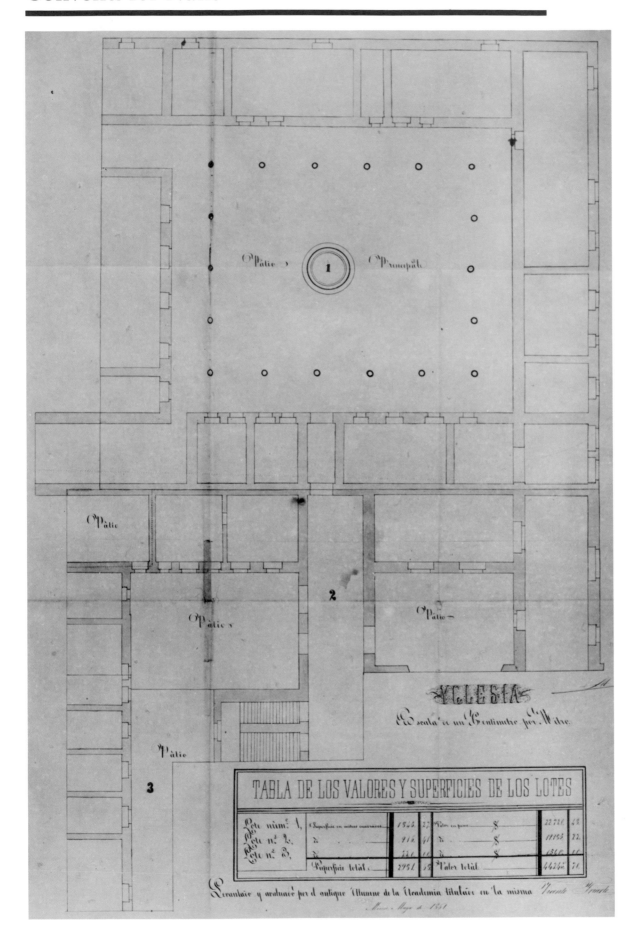

YGLESIA

Escala de un Centímetro por Metro

TABLA DE LOS VALORES Y SUPERFICIES DE LOS LOTES

This mid XIX century lithograph by Iriarte depicts the now lost cloister of Santa Isabel.
On the opposite page, Plan of one section of the convent, which was divided into three plots to be sold to private land owners. The box at the bottom shows the prices.

The Capuchinas Cloister in the process of being demolished in order to extend Palma Street.

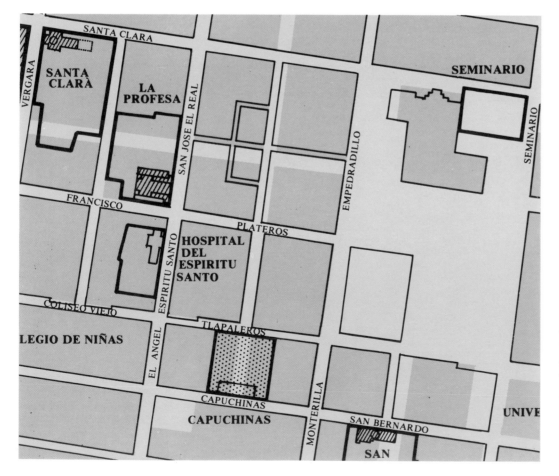

Location of the Capuchinas Convent. The street named after the convent is now part of Venustiano Carranza Street, between Isabel la Catolica (formerly Angel Street) and 5 de Febrero (formerly Monterilla Street). Tlapaleros Street is now called 16 de Septiembre.

Capuchinas

CONSECRATED IN 1673, ITS LONG HISTORY, beginning with the efforts of Captain Simon de Haro's widow, patron of La Concepcion, until its conclusion, can be found in the book *Mexican Throne,* by Brother Ignacio de la Peña (Madrid, 1728). The church was rebuilt between 1754 and 1756; architect Ildefonso de Iniesta Bejarano participated in the construction. During the XIX century, the interior of the church was given over to the Neoclassic style. The image of Our Lady of El Refugio was located behind the old church, placed there by Father Francisco Xavier Lazcano of the Society of Jesus. It gave its name to the street known as Refugio. Nothing remains of the Capuchinas Convent or Church.

Demolition of the Capuchinas Church and Convent, to extend Palma Street one short block to the south, between February and March, 1861.

Exterior of the Capuchinas Church. The marvelous balustered columns on its frontispiece and the beautiful image of San Felipe de Jesus, patron saint of the church, were completely destroyed along with the rest of the building.

Interior of the Capuchinas Church. Note the magnificent Neoclassic main altarpiece by Manuel Tolsa and the odd positioning of the lower choir, similar to that of La Enseñanza, and typical of Capuchinas convents in both Spain and Mexico. Lithograph from La Cruz, Mexico 1855.

Convents for Nuns

Cloister of the Corpus Christi Convent that escaped the Porfirian pickax but not the post revolutionary one.

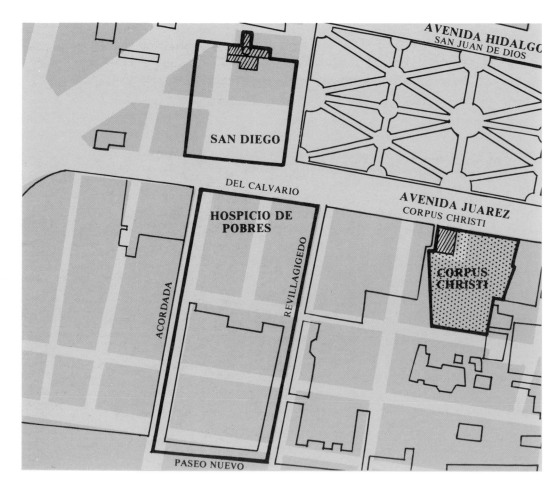

Location of the Corpus Christi Convent. The alley to the west of the church is now called Federico Garcia Lorca.

Corpus Christi

THIS CONVENT WAS FOR FRANCISCAN NUNS who were daughters of Indian caciques and was the result of the zeal of Viceroy Duke de Arion and Marquis de Valero, who laid the building's first stone in 1720. Josefina Muriel's detailed study of the building reports that this work by Pedro de Arrieta was rebuilt in 1750, by Brother Juan de Dios Rivera. Secularized like all other religious buildings in 1861, the nuns returned to their convent, during the Empire, but were forced to abandon it once again in 1867. The building became the property of Jose Ives de Limantour, who had it demolished, in order to build his home. The small remaining cloister was demolished in this century.

The church described by Rivera Cambas was still intact in 1880. During the twenties, Calles presented it to the schismatic patriarch, but the church failed and was converted into a warehouse. It then became a *souvenir shop* and, it is now a museum. Its wonderful XVIII century carved wooden doors were saved.

It is bizarre and grievous that this institution's church, which, in Josefina Muriel's words, represented, "the capacity of the indigenous spirit to reach the highest peaks of western culture", was turned into a Mexican handcrafts shop. All that was done to exalt the Indians during the XVIII century, became, in the XIX century, a symbol of their exploitation.

The current facade of the Corpus Christi Church. The surrounding buildings are in the process of being repaired as a consequence of the 1985 earthquakes.

129

A sculpture of San Agustin in the San Lorenzo Church. The monastic laws of San Agustin ruled the life of this community.

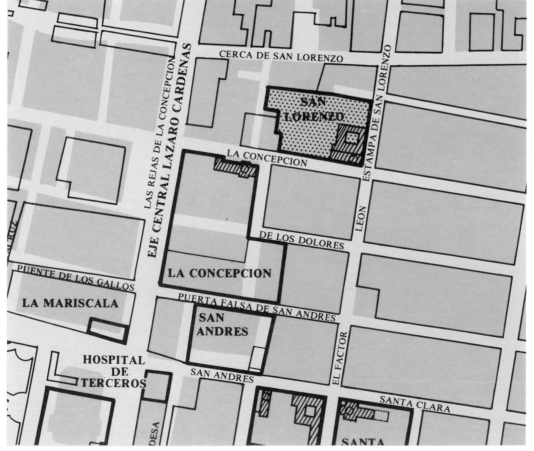

Location of the San Lorenzo Convent. Estampa de San Lorenzo Street is now a section of Allende Street. La Concepcion is now called Belisario Dominguez and Cerca de San Lorenzo is called Republica de Peru.

San Lorenzo

ALTHOUGH THEIR FOUNDING DATES BACK TO 1598, the San Lorenzo Church and Convent were not actually built until the mid XVII century, thanks to donations by don Juan de Chavarria y Valero and his wife, doña Maria Zaldivar Mendoza. According to many historians - Manuel Orozco y Berra, among others-, the church was consecrated in 1650. Nevertheless, an extremely rare pamphlet by Ignacio de Santa Cruz Aldana, printed by the heirs of Juan Ruiz in 1676, makes reference to the "happy renovation of the church and convent of the Lord of San Lorenzo of this Court". The pamphlet provides information on the altarpieces that were in the church, during the year of the supposed "happy renovation": *San Lorenzo*, the main one, was replaced in 1710 by the one by Manuel de Nava which was destroyed in the XIX century. *Santa Rosa de Lima; Prendimiento; Ecce Hommo; Presentacion; Guadalupe* and *San Jeronimo* were other altarpieces mentioned. In 1682, Manuel de Velazco was contracted to make the *Jueves Santo* Monument, and Juan de Chavarria y Valero bore the expense. Incidentally, the sketch of the latter's tomb in the church, drawn by Manuel Toussaint, survived, though the tomb itself did not. None of these pieces exist any longer. All the altarpieces and decorations referred to, were destroyed in the XIX century.

We must not overlook the church which was begun in 1643, and designed by Juan Gomez de Trasmonte and Juan Serrano. Likewise, we should not omit the great painting depicting the martyrdom of San Lorenzo, credited to Jose Juarez (though I believe it to be the work of Lopez de Arteaga), on the wall of the staircase leading from the lower to the upper cloister. It was rescued by Manuel Francisco Alvarez, who transformed the old convent into the Arts and Trades School. It later served as a barracks. Only a few walls of today's building are original. The church was saved, and its interior was modernized by Ertze Garamendi.

Detail on the San Lorenzo Church.

131

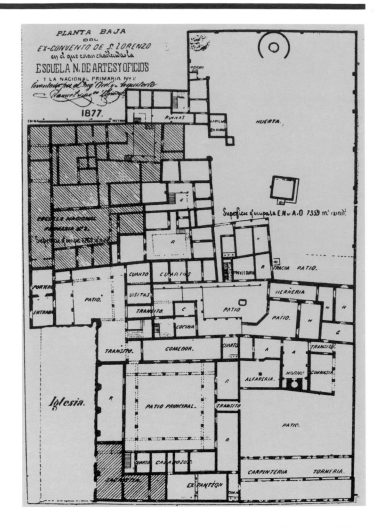

Plan by Manuel Francisco Alvarez that shows the ground floor of the convent before its transformation.

The cloister of San Lorenzo before it was demolished (1872). The sinking of the building can be clearly appreciated, thus revealing a certain degree of deterioration.

132

Plan of the same building after it was transformed.

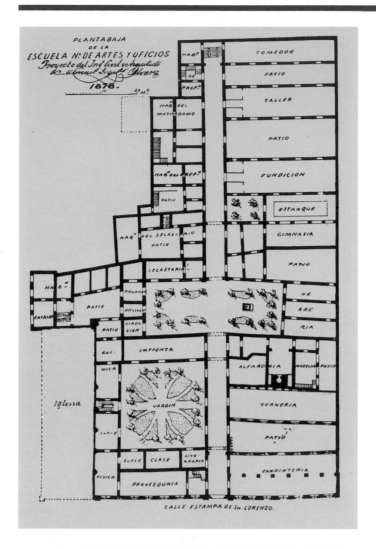

The San Lorenzo Cloister during its demolition (1875). Although the modifications made by Alvarez preserved all the buildings surrounding this courtyard, the demolition of the cloisters was deemed necessary.

Detail of the upper choir before it was destroyed.

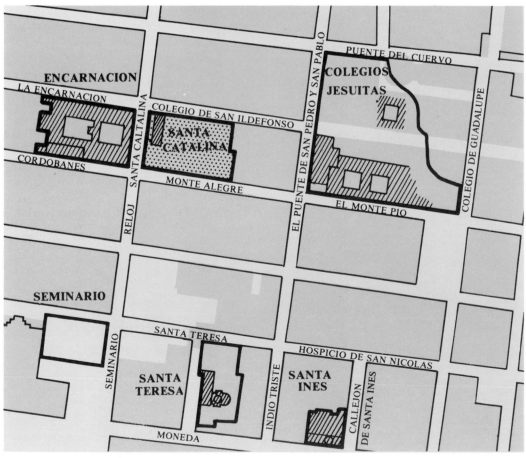

Location of the Santa Catalina Convent. The names Reloj and Santa Catalina were replaced by Republica de Argentina. Monte Alegre is now San Ildefonso.

Santa Catalina de Siena

SANTA CATALINA DE SIENA was founded in the XVI century. Three women, known as the Felipas, received backing from the Dominicans in Oaxaca to establish a convent for nuns of that order in Mexico City. Consequently, two nuns were sent to Mexico City from Antequera, that is, Oaxaca. The church was built between 1619 and 1623 and renovated in the XVIII century. Frontispieces and a tower were made, and everything except the choir was covered with vaults, and balustered altarpieces like the main one. In 1863, the nuns were secularized. From then on, the convent and church were damaged. The convent was partially demolished and used as a barracks. At a later date, it was turned into a law school.

The first part of the church to be demolished was its tower. According to Francisco de la Maza, it contained "several first rate altarpieces that were conserved until 1932", and referring to the very sad and senseless loss of the altarpieces, goes on to say:

> "... in those years, the Minister of Public Education was an illustrious Protestant whose hatred of Catholicism was exacerbated. Unable to bear seeing the Roman cult in front of his office, he decided to turn the church over to his Brothers. It was explained to him that, given the Lutheran iconoclasty, this change was not fitting, precisely on account of the altarpieces. He responded that they would all be respected, save the sculptures, which were replaced by signs with Biblical inscriptions on them. By 1936, not a single altarpiece remained. They were clandestinely and slowly dismantled and thrown into a warehouse"

Although the main altarpiece was later rescued, "the resting and rotting place" of the others is unknown.

Upper section of La Pasion Altarpiece, which no longer exists.

135

Above, the interior of the Santa Catalina de Siena Church in 1929.
Left, this altarpiece was fortunately installed in the Balvanera Chapel, a vestige of the San Francisco Convent, during the seventies.

The Interior of Santa Catalina which was used by the Presbyterian cult. Note the lattice work of the gallery at the end of the nave, a vestige of the extinct community of nuns.

The main altarpiece of Santa Catalina de Siena, with the signs placed by the Protestants instead of the original ornamented images. Were the workmen on the ladders the ones in charge of taking down the lateral piece?

Sagrado Corazon Altarpiece in the Santa Catalina Church. It stands where, in the previous photograph, the workmen's ladders were.

View of the nun's choir stalls at the beginning of the century. As we can see in this photograph, the use of Baroque fragments for a Neoclassic altarpiece, was extremely rare.

Pulpit and XVII century altarpiece in Santa Catalina. All gone.

Fragments of the previous altarpiece, when it was dismembered in the thirties, recognizable due to the picture frames.

Another view of the same disaster. The Descendimiento de la Cruz *oil painting is clearly shown in this photograph of the altarpiece, while it was still intact.*

Convents for Nuns

On the left, a lithograph of the Señor de Santa Teresa Chapel which shows the original cupola prior to the 1845 earthquake. On the right, a lithograph of the chapel after the earthquake.

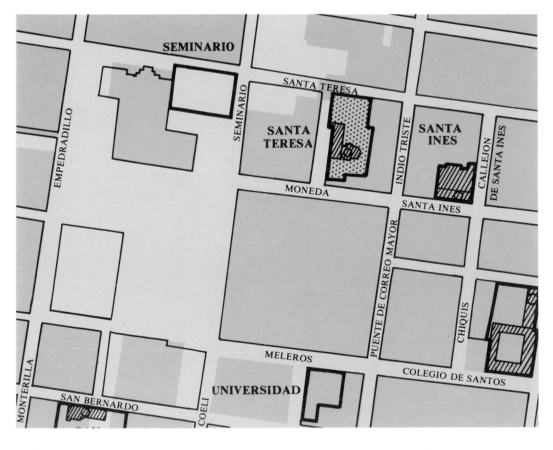

Location of the Santa Teresa Convent. Santa Teresa Street is now called Republica de Guatemala and Indio Triste is now El Carmen. Moneda Street still bears its original name, which has been changed on various occasions, to Arzobispado.

Santa Teresa la Antigua

THIS CONVENT WAS VERY IMPORTANT, however at the end of the XIX century, architect Manuel Francisco Alvarez demolished walls, archways and other buildings to turn it into the Normal School. The construction of the XVII church was due to its patron Esteban de Molina Mosquera who, around 1678, had the deed drawn up, entrusting the job to master architect Cristobal de Medina Vargas Machuca.

A Neoclassic chapel dedicated to the Señor de Santa Teresa was built next to the main church, and, among others, Patiño Ixtolinque and Ximeno y Planes were involved in its construction. The cupola and paintings, the work of the first generation of masters from the Academy, were lost in the 1845 earthquake. Nevertheless, the dome was rebuilt by Spanish architect Lorenzo de la Hidalga, and in the nineteen thirties it was made into an archive and storeroom, until it was recently rescued and restored.

The Señor de Santa Teresa Chapel before it became a warehouse. The marble domed structure was dismantled and is conserved, thanks to the Augustinians, in another church in Mexico City.

The second section of the Santa Brigida frontispiece. This solemn facade boasted the blazons of the founders of the community and, a niche with the image of Nuestra Señora de las Nieves, to whom the church was dedicated.

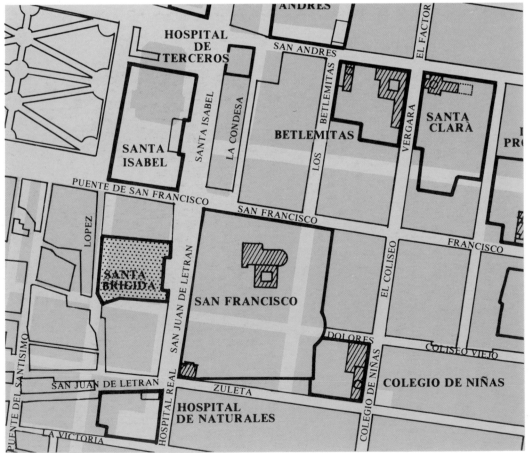

Location of the Santa Brigida Convent. The name San Juan de Letran lived on until a few years ago. Nowadays, this Avenue is known as Lazaro Cardenas or Central Thoroughfare, whereas, the street that runs along the back of the convent is still called Lopez, although nobody knows the origin of the name.

Santa Brigida

THIS CONVENT WAS BEGUN IN 1670 and finished in 1744. It took seventy seven years of paperwork to complete this project, started by don Francisco de Cordoba y Villafranca and his wife, a childless couple who decided to use their resources to support the nuns of the Order of the Saviour. The nuns were given a church that was unique in all of New Spain, because it had an elliptic floor plan, designed by engineer Luis Diez Navarro. The building never should have been touched, but the truth is, its destruction was due to the brilliant idea of expanding San Juan de Letran Street. At the time, some of the traffic problems were solved, but this did not last long. In exchange, we were left without this marvel.

The automobile has been one of the decisive factors in the destructive process of old cities. In the XXI century, there will be a different means of transportation, avenues may not even be needed and the last laugh will be on the ingenuous modernizers of our century who razed monuments to expand streets, considering it a sign of progress.

A corridor in the Santa Brigida Convent. When the expansion project for San Juan de Letran Street was announced, the proposal of moving the convent church stone by stone was rejected. There were no funds for the rescue.

Convents for Nuns

The exterior of Santa Brigida at the beginning of the XX century. Despite the fact that this same photograph was published in Doctor Atl's book Churches of Mexico *and that Justino Fernandez did a study of the building, it was lost as a result of public indifference.*

Demolition of the Santa Brigida Church in 1933. Its convent had suffered the same fate, and was demolished at the end of the XIX century, after having served as a military prison.

Betlemitas Cloister today. Note how the corridors have been invaded by low cost structures, in order to increase the number of housing units rented by the landlord.

X Hospitals and Schools

S PANISH DOMINATION OF AMERICA is fundamentally different from other historical colonization processes, because it was imbued with a redemptional zeal nourished by Catholic doctrine. This does not mean that it was above inflicting a good measure of atrocity upon the indigenous population, but it does explain why a vast and diverse social assistance project for the American population emerged from the very heart of Spanish society and its state. Although the attenuating effects of this project were ultimately limited, only in this way may we understand why so many charitable institutions were established in New Spain. The majority of these were hospitals and hospices. There were also elementary schools, boarding schools for orphans and abandoned children, lepers' hospitals, etcetera.

Hospitals were generally administered by the Hospitalers religious orders, which were similar to the Mendicant friars orders, although as well as the traditional vows of chastity, poverty and humility, its members were also bound by the obligation of caring for the needy. This meant that a hospital was not limited to caring for the sick or convalescents, but that it could also offer shelter to the destitute or travelers, whose situation was usually caused by circumstance rather than choice. At the beginning of the colonial era, the first evangelizing friars practised hospitality within their own institutions, as mentioned above. Consequently, the San Juan de Dios Order, with European origins, and the Nuestra Señora de Belem and San Hipolito Hospitalers orders, which were founded in the New World, began to work in New Spain. As a tremendous complement to all that the Church did through its religious institutions, charitable activities which were established and sponsored by private individuals, were administered by the clergy. In fact, the majority of the buildings we will deal with below, housed organizations of this kind.

The first stage in the scattering and eventual loss of the artistic treasure represented and gathered by these institutions, occurred with the extinction of the Hospitalers orders in the territories controlled by the Spanish Crown. This measure was decreed in 1820 by the Cadiz Courts, as a result of a process of secularization which stemmed from the Enlightenment, yet was never well received by the people of New Spain.

A more severe blow was undoubtedly dealt by the Reform Laws, the consequences of which affected medical assistance institutions, as well as schools, orphanages and other such organizations, which also came under

Above, a door in the interior of the San Ramon College. The coat-of-arms adorned with a cross and bars, identifies the members of the Mercedary order.
Left, interior of the Hospital de Naturales Chapel. It was first handed over to a Protestant sect and later, demolished.

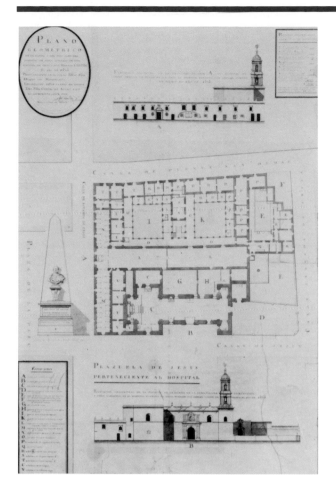

the Church's jurisdiction, and whose activities were to be strictly confined to spiritual matters. Exceptions to this rule are the San Ignacio College, better known as Vizcainas, which was founded by laymen and is therefore still in operation, and the Jesus Hospital, which continues to function, even though its building has suffered innumerable transformations.

The destructive process that has devastated some of the public assistance and school buildings will be illustrated in the following pages. In view of the disappearance of so many valuable buildings, the need to rescue the San Hipolito and Betlemitas Hospitaler buildings and give them a dignified and worthwhile use while ensuring their preservation, currently takes on a new sense of urgency.

Hospitals and Schools

The exterior of the Jesus Hospital before it was modified by the widening of Pino Suarez Street.

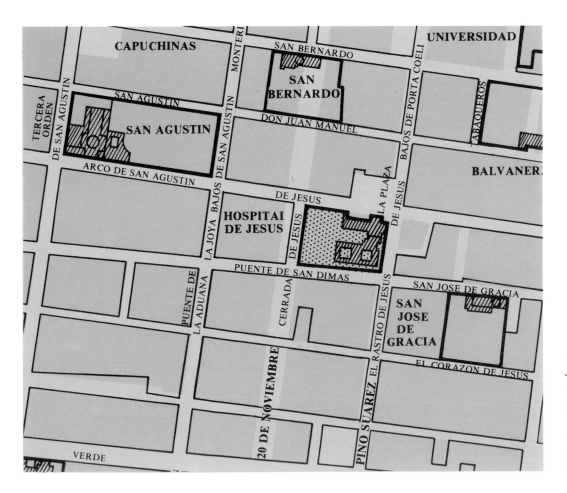

Location of the Jesus Hospital. Jesus Street now forms part of Republica de El Salvador. The square is named after Primo Verdad. Puente de San Dimas is now Mesones. The Jesus cul-de-sac was partially used to open up 20 de Noviembre Street.

Jesus Hospital

THE HISTORY OF THIS BUILDING is linked to that of its founder, Hernan Cortes. The marvelous book written by Eduardo Baez Macias on this important monument, provides the reader with a wealth of information. The church, started by Alonso Perez de Castañeda in 1601, remained unfinished for many years, until after winning a raffle, it received an image of Jesus of Nazareth donated by a rich Indian woman, Petronila Jeronima. The church was consecrated in 1665. In 1688, thanks to the patronage of Antonio Calderon Benavides, the wooden roofing of the vault was covered over. The altarpieces made by Antonio Maldonado, Tomas Juarez and Jose de Sayago date back to this period, and the sacristy still has its XVII century wooden coffering. Although the Hospitaler building has been modified, its XVI walls, adorned with fresco paintings are still intact. When Pino Suarez Street was broadened, the facade, which had also suffered certain modifications, was destroyed. The cloisters were encased by an outer shell, which in no way blended in with the antiquity of their walls. The church was renovated in 1835 and its interior decorated with Neoclassic altars, with no vestige of its former splendor remaining.

Current view of the hospital. A strip of the old building was demolished when Pino Suarez street was widened. This building was erected in order to increase the hospital's capacity. Behind it, the courtyards and other buildings of the old complex are still preserved.

153

Hospitals and Schools

Santa Paula Cemetery in 1855. San Fernando is the last remaining cemetery of that period in Mexico City.

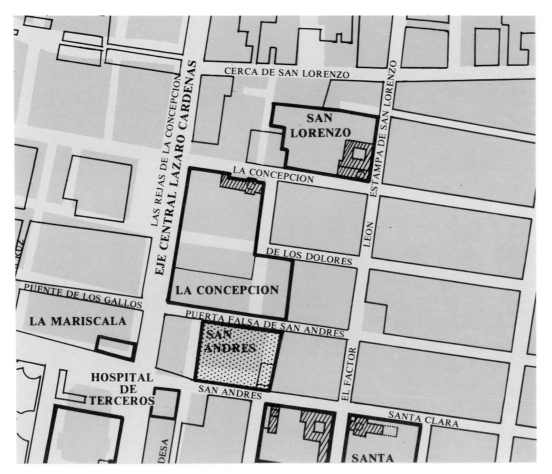

Location of the San Andres Hospital. San Andres Street is now known as Tacuba. La Puerta Falsa Street is now Donceles, and both names date back many years. Two new streets were opened up across the block; to the east, the extension of Filomeno Mata and to the west, Marconi.

San Andres and Santa Paula

IN HIS NOTES ON THE HISTORY OF SAN ANGEL, historian Francisco Fernandez del Castillo has gathered a considerable amount of information on the origins of the San Andres Novitiate, mainly due to the fact that its patrons were associated with the El Carmen Convent. At first it was known as Santa Ana, and after 1676, as San Andres. It began as a novitiate, later becoming a Jesuit school. The exercise house founded there was called De Aracoeli, and was consecrated in 1750. After the Jesuits had been expelled, Archbishop Nuñez de Haro y Peralta used the school as a hospital.

The church was built by Luis Gomez de Trasmonte around 1676, and in 1690, Antonio Maldonado was hired for its main altarpiece. The church began to deteriorate and was redecorated in the mid XVIII century. During the XIX century, it was once again refurbished, and in 1866, it was rebuilt only to be demolished in 1867, because Maximilian's wake was held there, thus making it a symbol of imperialism. Juan Jose Baz, a liberal politician who had previously promoted the destruction of the San Francisco Convent, obliterated it in one night. The exercise house became a tenement, and as already mentioned, the old school served as a hospital, until both were demolished at the end of the XIX century. The National Art Museum, a small street and the Senate Chamber, which still preserves some of the building's remains, now stand in its place.

The Santa Paula Cemetery was established in 1784 to provide service to the old San Andres Hospital. It was essentially an open area with a small chapel, surrounded by a wall. In 1836, City Hall turned it into the Main Cemetery. The following year, it was embellished considerably, when streets with balustrades, flowers, bushes and trees, such as cypresses, pines and cedars, were added. A pamphlet published in 1852 contains a register of all the people buried there, including the Count de Regla, Melchor Muzquiz, several heroes from the 1847 war and Diego Garcia Conde. It no longer exists, as it was razed during the last third of the XIX century. The leg of Antonio Lopez de Santa Anna was once buried there.

Hospitals and Schools

Tacuba Street at the beginning of the XX century. The old Jesuit complex can be seen, although without its church. The hospital was the fifth building from the corner.

The exterior of the San Andres Hospital. Immediately to the right, the Exercise House (1890).

To the right, a current view of the same corner. Further down the street, the Manuel Tolsa Square now lies where the old Baroque Jesuit Hospital once stood.
Below, the courtyard of the San Andres Hospital, which disappeared without leaving a trace (1890).

The Cemetery Chapel in 1860. The sculptures represent the theological virtues of faith, hope and charity.

The same chapel one hundred years later. Nowadays, it only has youngsters perched on its buttresses. Shortly after the extension of Reforma Avenue extension, at its juncture with Rayon, the church disappeared.

Hospitals and Schools

An 1853 watercolor showing the Betlemitas Church and, in the background, San Andres before it was demolished.

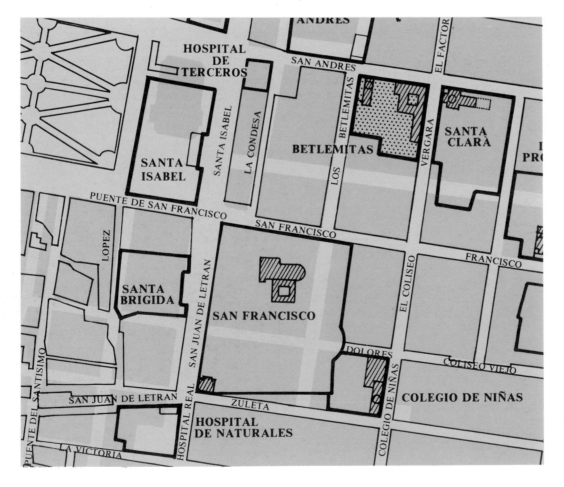

Location of the Betlemitas Hospital. Betlemitas Alley is now known as Filomeno Mata; Vergara is called Bolivar, and San Andres, Tacuba.

Betlemitas

THE BETLEMITAS HOSPITALER ORDER was established in Guatemala by Pedro de San Jose Vetancourt. The hospital they founded in Mexico was begun in 1675 and concluded in 1754; the church was opened in 1687. Around 1754, this extraordinary complex included a school for 800 students, yet, was nevertheless unjustly ruined and modified. At one time, the church had wonderful altarpieces, as shown in a painting by Carlos de Villalpando, now housed in the Tepotzotlan Museum. Laureano Ramirez de Contreras created the main altarpiece, and Manuel de Velazco made some of the lateral pieces. The hospital was the work of Lorenzo Rodriguez. Its courtyard is certainly one of his greatest accomplishments. The church has served as the warehouse of the former Development Secretariat, a technological museum, an economics and social science library and currently houses a military museum. The old hospital was partially demolished -Manuel Romero Rubio, Secretary of the Interior from 1884 to 1895, built his house on part of the site- and the remaining structure now functions as a tenement. It is currently being further ruined by the indifference of city dwellers and the commercial zeal of its owners.

The old Betlemitas Alley which is now Filomeno Mata. The atrium of the chapel, which can be seen on the right, was partially invaded, resulting in the demolition of the tower and the bell tower.

161

Interior of the Betlemitas Church; oil painting.

A view of the chapel when it was adapted for one of its many uses.

Around the decade of the sixties, the project for widening this street was announced, as formerly occurred with Pino Suarez, San Juan de Letran and Izazaga. It was only thanks to the decisive and energetic protests of a civil society, that the project was eventually suspended.

The triumphal arch, built in honor of Empress Charlotte (1864). To the left, we can see the atrium wall of San Andres, as well as a fragment of the Aracoeli Exercise House. On the right, the old Betlemitas Hospital, with its chapel in the foreground.

Hospitals and Schools

The doorway of the Naturales Hospital.

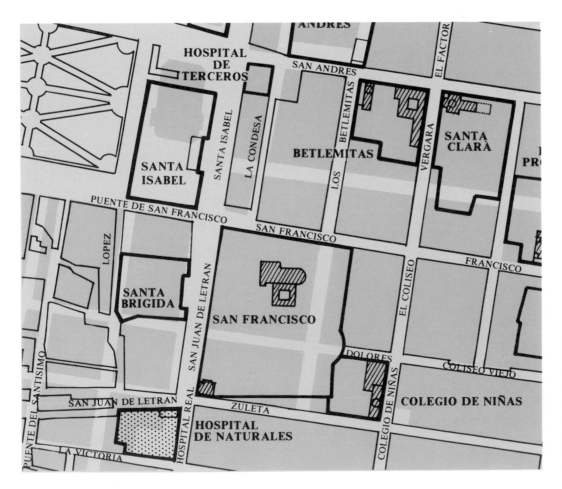

Location of the Naturales Hospital. The old name, Hospital Real referred to the institution's complete name. The street is now the Central Thoroughfare. The gray shadow indicates an open square where there was once a building that was damaged in the 1985 earthquakes.

Real de Naturales Hospital

THE ESTABLISHMENT OF THIS HOSPITAL dates back to the era of Carlos V. During the XVII century, it obtained part of its income from the theatrical activities carried out there. In the XVIII century, it occupied an area which measured 246 varas in length, by 89 wide at the facade and 71 to the west. Of its eight rooms, some were more than one hundred varas long. In 1768, practical anatomy classes were started and imparted by professor Antonio Martinez y Virgili. Virtually the entire building was given to printer Ignacio Cumplido, who lived there until 1880, the year of his death. It was demolished to permit the widening of San Juan de Letran.

The building's courtyard after it ceased to be used as a hospital.

Hospitals and Schools

The exterior of the Real de Naturales Hospital in the nineteen twenties.

Frontispiece of the Real de Naturales Hospital. Rescued by Finance Secretary, Luis Montes de Oca, it now forms part of a house in San Angel.

The main courtyard of the Naturales Hospital.

Demolition of the Hospital during the nineteen thirties.

Hospitals and Schools

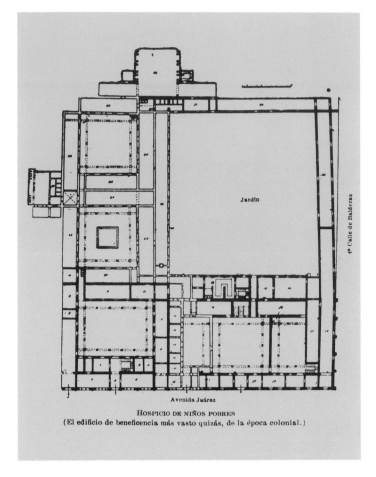

HOSPICIO DE NIÑOS POBRES
(El edificio de beneficencia más vasto quizás, de la época colonial.)

Plan of the Hospice for the Poor (1856).

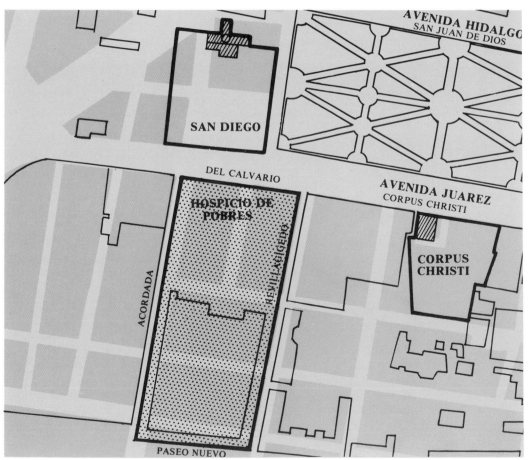

Location of the Hospice for the Poor. The only name that survived was that of Revillagigedo, the Viceroy who allowed this zone to be desiccated to permit the expansion of the city. Acordada Street is now the considerably wider Balderas, and Calvario Street has become Juarez Avenue.

Hospice for the Poor

THE HOSPICE FOR THE POOR, which was the largest colonial public assistance institution, was once located on what is now Juarez Avenue, alongside old Acordada Street. This outstanding building was unveiled in 1744, thanks to the efforts of don Fernando Ortiz Cortes, precentor of Mexico City Cathedral. Around 1798, don Francisco Zuñiga ordered the construction of a separate building for children, to avoid them mingling with the rest of the poor. The new establishment, called Patriotica School, was opened in 1806 and linked to the Hospice for the Poor. Joaquin Garcia Icazbalceta provides us with information on the condition of the building in 1806, in a text presented to Emperor Maximilian by Jose Maria Andrade and published by Luis Garcia Pimentel in 1907. Thanks to this text, we have an idea of the importance of this enormous building and the stupidity of allowing it to be demolished.

The exterior of the Hospice for the Poor and the Patriotica School (1855).

169

Hospitals and Schools

A panoramic view of the city in 1860, with the cupola, vault and bell tower of the Espiritu Santo Hospital, in the foreground. We can see that the church's nave ran parallel to the street, as was often the case with nuns' convents. To the left, the towers of La Profesa, and in the background, Santo Domingo.

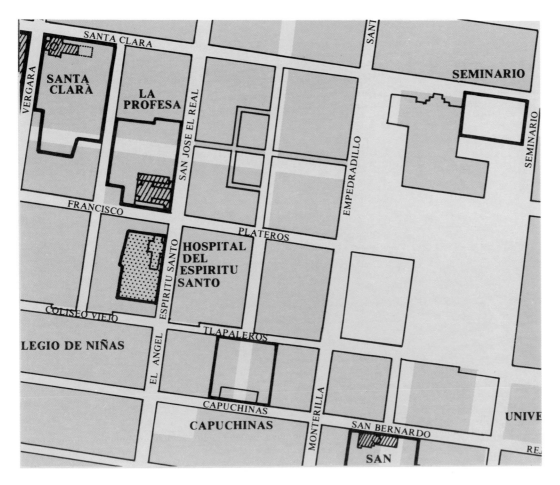

Location of the Espiritu Santo Hospital. The street that once bore the hospital's name is now the section of Isabel la Catolica that lies between Madero (formerly San Francisco) and 16 de Septiembre (formerly Coliseo Viejo) streets.

Espiritu Santo Hospital

DUE TO THE ENDOWMENT PROVIDED by don Alonso Rodriguez de Vado and his wife, doña Ana Zaldivar, the Espiritu Santo Hospital was begun during the first half of the XVII century. It remained in the hands of the Hypolites until the Cadiz Courts suppressed the Hospitaler orders in 1820. The Hospital, convent and church were all rebuilt at the end of the XVII century.

The church was consecrated in the following century, on May 19, 1715. During the XIX century, the building housed the School of Medicine and a printer's shop. The latter occurred as the result of a decree, which granted the building to Vicente Garcia Torres on October 15, 1842, who only partially occupied it. The Baroque church was one of the most beautiful in the city, above all because of its tower and its dome. The whole complex disappeared during the second half of the XIX century.

On the left, we can see the sidewalk of Espiritu Santo Street on which the hospital was located. In the center, hemmed in by the alignment of the street and surrounded by parasitic structures, the wall of the church's cross vault can barely be seen (1875). Today, the Casino Español sits in its place. On the right, we can appreciate a detail of the church's heavy decoration of small lanterns and skylights that take us back to the XVIII century Baroque.

Hospitals and Schools

The Hospital de Terceros Court-yard (c. 1890).

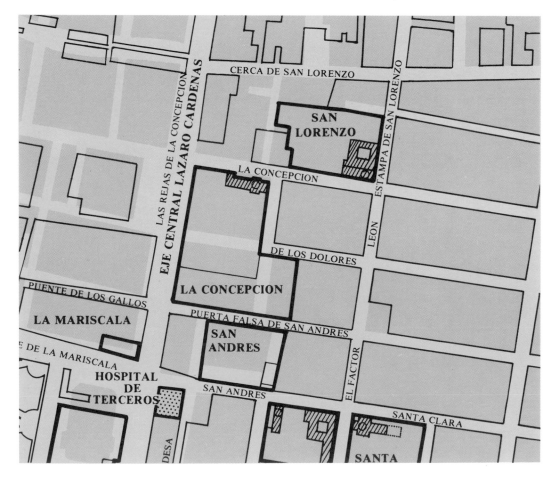

Location of the Terceros Hospital. The alley is still called La Condesa, whereas San Andres and Santa Isabel have been turned into Tacuba Street and Lazaro Cardenas Thoroughfare, respectively.

Terceros Hospital

After its establishment in 1615, the Franciscan Third Order founded its chapel in the San Francisco de Mexico Convent. The first building was constructed during the second half of the XVII century and the second one around 1720. In 1750, Fernando VI gave authorization for the members of the order to found a hospital in Mexico City. Work was begun on the old site of the Villegas Estate and was finally opened in 1756.

After the Reform, the building was sold, and in its place, the Ferrocarril Inn was established. During the years of the Empire, it was used for the offices of the Finance and War Secretariat, with its corresponding Court Martial section. After 1867, the School of Commerce and the Mexican Society of Geography and Statistics took up residence in the building. In 1900, the building was demolished for the construction of the Central Post Office, a pseudo-Gothic building by Italian Adamo Boari.

The facade of the Hospital de Terceros, while still intact. The ground floor windows were later blocked off.

The Terceros Hospital as seen in an 1861 lithograph. The tree grove in the background is the Alameda Park.

Above, the Terceros Hospital, as seen in a late XIX century photograph. On the far right is the Mining Palace.

On the right, three of the great buildings from the era of Porfirio Diaz - the Fine Arts Palace, the current National Art Museum and the Central Post Office - implied the total obliteration of many viceregal buildings. In this case, only the corner of the Mining Palace, visible in the left hand side of the photograph, shows that we are dealing with the same place.

175

Hospitals and Schools

Panoramic view, showing the unique arches of the Girls School, which stand out over the city's rooftops. On the left, we can see the school's chapel, which is now dedicated to Our Lady of Lourdes. In the background, the main San Francisco Church, with its bell tower still intact, and the groves of the Alameda Park can be appreciated.

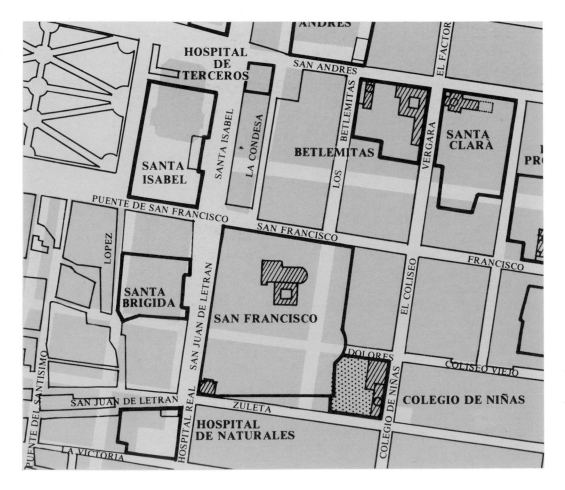

Location of the Girls School. The corner of Zuleta and Colegio de Niñas in now called Venustiano Carranza and Bolivar. The names Coliseo and Coliseo Viejo refer to the theaters that were on these streets from viceregal times.

Girls School

FORMERLY KNOWN as the Santa Maria de la Caridad College, this magnificent complex still exists, despite the fact that it has been defaced and altered. During the XVII and XVIII centuries, the church's interior was magnificent. The lavish Churrigueresque work on the lateral pieces by Felipe de Ureña (1742), was lost with the Neoclassic decor of the XIX century. The School had an extremely sober exterior that was modified when it became the Colon Theater. Recently, its current owner, a true businessman, tried to modernize the exterior, but was prevented from doing so by the Colonial Monuments Department.

The facade of the Girls School in 1880, although without its large fortified tower and with other minor alterations. Nevertheless, it still retains some of its original character.

The Girls School is shown here in the center of the photograph, as yet without the modifications it received during the period following disentailment. Photograph dating from 1860.

The present surroundings of the Girls School. The building served as the Colon Theater for many years, and it was during this period that the facade was transformed as all of the windows it has today were created.

Hospitals and Schools

The old courtyard of San Ramon College.

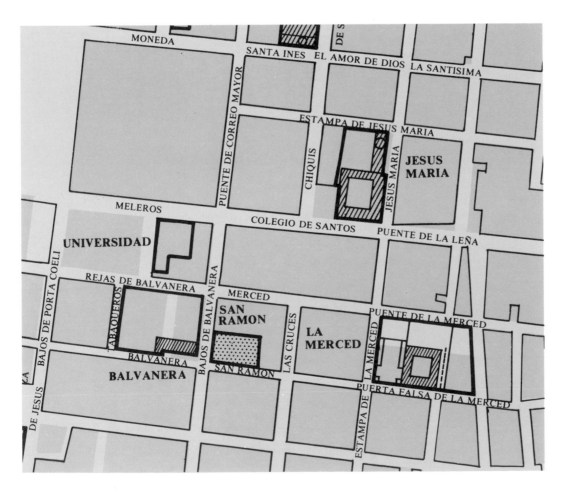

Location of San Ramon College. The corner of Bajos de Balvanera and San Ramon is currently known as Correo Mayor and Republica de Uruguay, respectively. The name Las Cruces still exists.

San Ramon College

ESTABLISHED IN 1654, the Comendadores Juristas de San Ramon College became part of the college of San Juan de Letran when it could no longer support itself with its own resources. It was on the corner of Primera de San Ramon (currently Uruguay) and Correo Mayor. The building remained intact until the nineteen thirties, when it was demolished, and only its frontispiece was conserved.

The exterior of San Ramon College.

Besides the frontispiece shown here, a few of the doors that appear in the photograph on the opposite page can still be seen in the interior of this building.

The magnificent cupola of the Loreto Church, as seen from a now disappeared staircase. The Jesuits introduced the capital of New Spain to the cult of Our Lady of Lourdes.

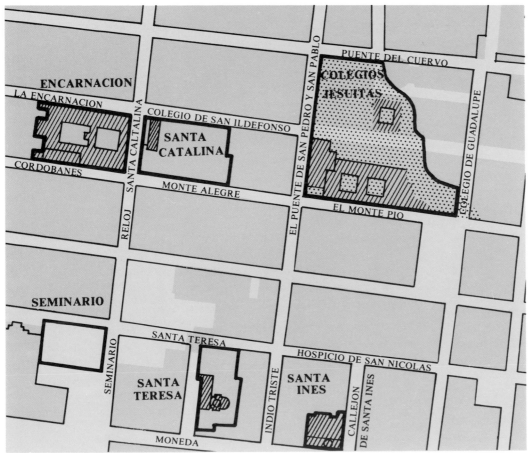

Location of the Jesuit schools. One of these schools gave the name of Puente de San Pedro y San Pablo to the street that is now known as Del Carmen. Puente del Cuervo is currently called Republica de Colombia. El Monte Pio is now San Ildefonso.

Jesuit Schools

UPON THEIR ARRIVAL IN NEW SPAIN IN 1572, the Jesuits lodged at the Jesus Hospital and the San Agustin Convent in Mexico City. They obtained a piece of land on which they constructed the building that would serve as their study center, later known as the Maximo de San Pedro y San Pablo College. During their first decade they established study programs, gained prestige within the community and became involved in a number of controversies with the Dominicans and the University. The church was built on land belonging to the wealthy miner Alonso de Villaseca, who donated 90 thousand pesos for the construction and consequently became its patron. The church was consecrated in 1603. It was initially decorated with Renaissance-style altarpieces, which were gradually replaced by Baroque altarpieces, created during the XVIII century by the Indian sculptor Tomas Juarez, as well as several balustered columns, the work of Isidoro Vicente de Balbas (XVIII century). The school had a magnificent library which was later scattered. Carlos de Siguenza y Gongora bequeathed all his papers on old Mexico, his volumes of the works of Father Anastasio Kircher and even some mammoth bones to this library. Documents from the Temporalities branch of the General Archives of the Nation and other papers, copies of which are currently in the hands of the learned Jesuit Manuel Ignacio Perez Alonso, give us an idea of how rich this school was. To the east, the San Gregorio School and the Loreto Chapel completed this enormous Jesuit citadel. The Lauretana Chapel, described by Father Francisco de Florencia in the XVII century, was renovated in the XVIII century and demolished in the XIX, to make way for a building by Agustin de Paz, a student of Manuel Tolsa, which was financed by Count Bassoco. One block west, another Jesuit building was constructed, San Ildefonso College, which was completely rebuilt between 1712 and 1740.

This building complex has undergone a wide range of changes, and although it has avoided total ruin, it was nonetheless looted during the XVIII century, after the expulsion of the Jesuits from Spanish domains in 1767. Jose Vasconcelos, among others, was especially concerned about giving the building a dignified use related to its original purpose, that of study and teaching. This example alone is sufficient to show what might have been done with the enormous building complexes that belonged to religious orders. They could have been dedicated to culture instead of being demolished.

Hospitals and Schools

The interior of the San Pedro y San Pablo Church stripped of its altarpieces as a result of the expulsion of the Jesuits. Among its other uses, it served as the seat of Congress during the early years of Mexican independence.

The opening of Venezuela Street. This street was extended eastward, cutting across the Jesuit school buildings.

The San Pedro y San Pablo Church, with murals by Roberto Montenegro. This building was used as the National Newspaper Library until the nineteen seventies.

Current view of Venezuela Street as seen from the Abelardo L. Rodriguez Market. Part of one of the Jesuit courtyards was incorporated into the market building.

Conclusion

WHENEVER THE BAROQUE DREAM OF NEW SPAIN, from within its isolation, adopted outside forms, it adapted them and made them its own. As of the Enlightenment, at the end of the XVIII century, the past began to be considered as something dark and barbaric, in comparison with the brilliance of civilization. The prevailing sentiment was that change could not come from within, but rather from abroad, from the future. Suddenly, the Baroque tradition became something shameful and reprehensible.

The age of imitation commenced. Creativity ground to a standstill and everything possible was done to imitate. Thus emerged the need to compare our reality with that of the outside world, which claimed to represent the essence of perfection: a model. In the aftermath of revolution, and to some extent, even before, France became a model for Spain and its colonies. Propaganda was so effective and the Hispanic decadence of the previous century so marked, that the disavowal of its originality was inevitable. Spain taught us this lesson when it ceased to be an empire and became a sort of French province, relinquishing the characteristics of its Golden Century. The distinctive forms that expressed the diverse uniqueness of its universal isolation began to disappear, when an attempt was made to emulate the model imposed by the enlightened character of the Bourbon monarchy. In the Hispanic world, the learned elements of society obliterated the Baroque and with it its great art.

An attempt was made at homogenization in the colonies, which denied their diversity of expression and form. The colonies wished for modernity, regardless of the cost, imitating the more advanced countries, as did the Messianic and Napoleonic gestures of their rulers, during the early years of Independence. Everything from furniture to laws were fashioned in accordance with these models. Nothing was derived from our own tradition, but rather from an alien present, as we did not dare to live and create our own. Creative impulse gave way to imitation.

Initially comparison, and then imitation provoked the demise of the originality and specific nature of our works. To make a comparison implies measuring one thing against another, yet the supposition that one of the two is the model is also inherent. XIX century Europe, and later America, with their ideals and novelties, imposed themselves on the entire world as models to be imitated. Mexico was no exception. This devastating and standardizing foreign influence has been felt all the way from Latin America to Cairo. All original expression was conceived as being valueless, and any sign of uniqueness regarded as a lack of civilization, except by the Romantics who, in the end, were defeated by the Positivists.

Imitation implies seeking a likeness with something. Comparison and imitation form an implacable binomial against criticism and originality. A comparison or imitation occurs when it is naively, and sometimes correctly

Conclusion

believed that anything from abroad is better. When one thing is compared to another and it is believed that one is superior to the other, then any difference is conceived as an error. Attention is fixed on identical features, and not on what is different, on similarity, rather than dissimilarity.

Criticism is practically the opposite of comparison. To criticize is to discern, distinguish, separate one thing from another, in order to evaluate it from its own center of gravity. Criticism presumes criterion, discretion, or the ability to understand, which is not the same as comparing. Imitation is almost an animal characteristic, whereas originality is something human. To criticize implies a greater mental activity than that used for comparison. When criticizing, one seeks something different, while with comparison, there is a search for identical elements. Imitation is like the child of criticism that demands its distinction. Those who follow trends lack this elective faculty, which is why they are never elegant. Trends are preferred by those who lack originality, or in other words, lack origin, and because they do not know where to go, they imitate.

To create is to give life, a solution to the encounter of the old with the new. When the past is flatly denied and only exogenous features are perceived and expected, from abroad and from the future, then only imitation is produced. On the other hand, when the past is discerned, and only the best is taken for one's self-assertion in the encounter of the new, without breaking the link with the old, it is possible to derive a solution from one's origin and therefore achieve originality, which means taking care of what is truly ours. Originality and criticism are always linked to liberty and consciousness; comparison and imitation, however, are always related to dependence and backwardness. Anyone pursuing a model to compare himself with, always arrives late and never achieves the desired autonomy, because he assumes that change comes from without, and not from within.

In Mexico, during the XIX century, both spiritual and material destruction took place. Damage was inflicted upon both space and time. Under the seductive, charismatic and guileful Santa Anna, we lost half of our territory, consisting of soil and space, and with don Porfirio Diaz, hieratic, solemn and monumental, we lost our past, which was our origin and time. Until the triumph of the 1857 Republic, we really suffered a great material disaster, due to the absence of a clearly defined attitude regarding the present, in relation to the past and the future, which placed our sovereignty at considerable risk. Personal ambitions, political disorder and neglect of our heritage were some of the causes that encouraged the material disaster. Everyone agreed to deny the past. The conservatives dreamt about Europe and constitutional monarchies and the liberals about the United States and the modern republics. By denying our roots and starting from scratch, comparative attitudes and imitative aspirations were encouraged.

As of 1867, material conditions improved, yet the ontological ones worsened. During the following years, and above all during the era of Porfirio Diaz, the "progress" fever broke out, which literally meant "imitation". Everything was expected from abroad, from outside, and from the future. During the Porfiriato, the past was snatched away. Our indigenous heritage was exaggerated and exalted, because it was remote and harmless -it was a question of a dead Indian- and was treated with aseptic and scientific aims. Everything pertaining to New Spain was reduced to picturesque and bizarre tales, which were filled with rogues, buccaneers, swordsmen and ambushes. The immediate past, that of the XIX century itself, was used as far as possible, as a pedestal of the glory that don Porfirio built for himself. Generally speaking, our "National History" became transformed into a series of facts that led to the recognition of the greatness of the dictatorship. The Porfiriato was a cunning recorder of the past, the creator of "the bronze history", which was unable to withstand "the national novelty" produced by the Revolution, which, as Lopez Velarde said, now aspired to a more modest nation and for this very reason, a more precious one. The Porfirio Diaz era with its positivist philosophy sought to "know in order to foresee", yet not to understand the country: imitating to make progress.

Nevertheless, the legacy of the official history fabricated during the Porfiriato is somehow still valid. The impetuous, ceremonious, anachronistic and misleading civil gestures have something of a Porfirian air, and the aversion to, or censure of certain periods of the past and their cultural and artistic expressions, which benefited the social sciences and economics, have a positivistic and "scientific" smell and taste about them. The first thing that the Revolution did was to attempt to recover the inner nature, the past and the originality of our being. Its advocates had the vision, passion and tenderness to rejoice in the magnificence of Mexico. Men such as Jose Vasconcelos, Genaro Estrada or Dr. Atl, who once again had eyes for the style of New Spain, its popular art and until then, shameful past. The men of the Porfirio Diaz era, were so confident of the outside world and the future, so sure of their project and desire for progress, that they were completely taken aback when they realized that change was being produced from within, from the memory and authenticity, constantly threatened by deceit and disguise. The Revolution of 1910 was a cultural upheaval that allowed Mexico to see its past and reality through different eyes, the eyes of comprehension and love.

Nonetheless, comparative attitudes and imitative gestures have begun to re-emerge with all imaginable impetus. So far, it has not been possible to establish the necessary continuity to allow the attitudes and ideas of the 1910 cultural revolution to be assimilated. Likewise, there has been no active expression to correct all that our country suffered in terms of its past and its originality. Once again, society does not know what to do with its past, which, on the few occasions when it is not abducted by bureaucrats who behave like the owners of the nation, gets in the way and causes embarrassment. When civil society attempts to do something, it is subtly harassed and impotently watches the process of damage and deterioration suffered by its heritage and monuments.

The destruction of monuments has been a sadly common task, a process involving many sectors of the population. There is one essential reason for this: a lack of love and interest in all that we call our own, which causes passiveness and forgetfulness, disdain and strangeness. Dependence and backwardness are covered up by the desire to imitate and compare and the false expectations of all that is alien to us. Change comes both from within and without, and originality is the solution to this challenging encounter. The conservation of monuments is in itself, an affirmation of nationality, a means of safeguarding its memory in order to orient its project. This is not an isolated task, but rather the expression of a being that must continually gain strength. While it fails to be completely understood as something more than mere nostalgia, but rather as one of the most significant acts of a society graced with consciousness, then we shall continue to impotently witness the passiveness of different sectors of society that do nothing to prevent the deterioration of our monuments. Conscience and liberty produce criticism and originality; comparison and imitation, dependence and backwardness.

Onomastic and Toponymical Index

A

Acordada Street: 169
Adriano, Brother Juan: 10
Agueda de San Ignacio, Mariana: 85
Alcantara, Juan de: 55
Aldana, Ignacio de Santa Cruz: 131
Alvarez, Manuel Francisco: 131
America: 187
Anaya, Francisco Antonio de: 55, 73
Andrade, Jose Maria: 169
Angeles, Blas de los: 65
Antequera, Oaxaca: 135
Aora, Juan de: 9
Aracoeli, Exercise House: 155
Aranzazu Chapel: 10, 16
Arciniega, Claudio de: 9, 10, 55
Architecture Division of the National Institute of Fine Arts: 121
Arion, Marquis of Valero and Viceroy Duke of: 129
Arjona Montalvo, Francisco: 14
Armella de Aspe, Virginia: 81
Arrieta, Pedro de: 16, 55, 81, 129
Arts and Trades School: 131
Atlixco, Puebla: 117
Austin Library: 16

B

Baez Macias, Eduardo: 16, 153
Balbas, Isidoro Vicente de: 55, 121, 183
Balbas, Jeronimo de: 16, 87
Balvanera Convent: 83, 99ss
Balvanera Chapel: 10, 16
Bassoco, Count: 183
Baz, Juan Jose: 155
Becerra, Francisco:10, 55
Berlin, Enrique: 55
Betlemitas College: 11
Betlemitas Hospital: 151, 161ss
Bibliography of the Art of New Spain: 107
Boari, Adamo: 173
Borondate, Guillermo: 73
Bourbon monarchy: 187
Buen Tono Church: 117, 119

C

Cabello, Feliciano: 16
Cabrera, Miguel: 16, 81
Cadiz Courts: 149, 171
Cairo: 187
Calderon Benavides, Antonio: 153
Calderon de la Barca,

Marchioness: 95
Calvario Highway, old: 15
Cambas Rivera: 129
Capuchinas Convent: 83, 125ss.
Carillo y Perez, Ignacio: 17
Carlos V: 13, 165
Carmelite Order: 10
Casela, Jose: 95
Castillo, Diego del: 121
Cathedral of Mexico City: 9, 13, 16, 169
Catholic, Genteel and Political Mexico: 17
Central Post Office: 173
Cervantes de Salazar, Francisco: 9, 13
City Hall: 155
City Hall Records: 9
Colon Theater: 177
Colonial Monument Department: 177
Concha, Andres de la: 65
Constanso, Manuel: 95
Consulado Chapel: 14
Cordoba y Villafranca, Francisco de: 145
Corpus Christi Convent: 83, 129ss.
Correo Mayor Street: 181
Cortes, Hernan: 13,153
Couto, Jose Bernardo: 81
Court Martial: 173
Covarrubias, Nicolas de: 107
Coyoacan, town of: 119
Cruz, Jose Antonio de la: 15, 65
Cruz, Pedro de la: 13
Cruz, Sor Juana Ines de la: 85
Culhuacan Altarpiece: 14
Cumplido, Ignacio: 165
Chapultepec Castle: 119
Charreria Museum: 79
Chauvet, Fidel: 17
Chavarria y Valero, Juan de: 65, 131
Chavez, Higinio de : 16
Chavez, Mateo de: 99
Cholula Chapel: 16
Christ College: 14
Churubusco Convent: 121

D

De Profundis Room: 9
Development Secretariat: 161
Dialogue on Painting in Mexico: 81
Diaz Porfirio: 188
Diez Navarro, Luis: 145
Dorta, Marco: 55
Dr. Atl: 189

E

Ecce Hommo Altarpiece: 131
Echave Orio, Baltazar de: 13, 15, 81
El Calvario: 13
El Carmen Square: 10
Espinosa, Simon de: 65
Espiritu Santo Hospital: 171ss
Estrada Genaro: 189
Europe: 187, 188

F

Felipe II: 91
Fernandez del Castillo, Francisco: 155
Fernando VI: 173
Ferrocarril Inn: 173
Finance and War Secretariat: 173
Fine Arts Palace: 121
France: 187
Fuentes, Andres de: 14

G

Gante, Pedro de: 9, 13
Garamendi, Ertze: 131
Garcia Conde, Diego: 155
Garcia Cubas, Antonio: 17
Garcia Guerra, Archbishop: 103
Garcia Izcalbalceta, Joaquin: 169
Garcia Pimentel, Luis: 169
Garcia Torres, Vicente: 171
General Archives of the Nation: 9, 11 , 87, 183
Generalito, El: 65
Gil, Jeronimo Antonio: 16
Girls School: 177ss.
Gomez de Orozco, Federico: 17
Gomez de Trasmonte, Luis: 155
Gomez de Trasmonte, Juan: 87
Gonzalez Beascoechea, Manuel: 55
Gonzalez, Diego: 107
Gonzalez Velazquez, Jose Antonio: 91
Granada. Spain: 81
Great O.H.F. Francisco de Mexico Convent: 13
Guadalupe Altarpiece: 131
Guatemala: 161
Guerrero y Torres, Francisco de: 97

H

Hagenbeck: 111
Hapsburg, Maximillian of, Emperor of Mexico: 155, 169
Haro, Simon de: 125
Heredia, Francisco de: 13
Heredia, Mateo de: 13
Holy Register: 107
Hospice for the Poor: 169ss
Hospitals and Schools: 149ss.
Hypolites: 171

I

Imperial Santo Domingo de Mexico Convent: 55ss.

Iniesta Bejarano, Ildefonso de: 125
Izazaga Street:: 79

J

Jaspers socle: 13
Jesus de la Penitencia: 99
Jesus Hospital: 151, 153ss., 183
Jesus Maria Convent: 83
Jesus Maria Royal Monastery: 91ss.
Jesus of Nazareth, image of: 153
Juarez Avenue: 15, 169
Juarez, Jose: 81, 131
Juarez, Tomas: 55, 65, 73, 153, 183,
Jueves Santo Monument: 131
Justo Sierra Street:: 65

K

Kircher, Anastacio: 183

L

La Concepcion Convent: 83, 87ss., 125
La Encarnacion Convent: 83, 95ss.
La Encarnacion Monastery: 95
La Enseñanza Antigua Convent: 83
La Enseñanza Nueva Convent: 83
La Merced Convent: 10
La Merced Order: 10
La Casa Profesa of the Society of Jesus: 10, 81ss.
Latin America: 187
Lauretana Chapel: 183
Lavarriere, Julio: 73
Lazcano, Francisco Xavier: 125
Leandro Valle Street: 55
Life in Mexico: 95
Limantour, Jose Ives: 129
Lopez de Arteaga: 131
Lopez Morillo, Diego: 13
Lopez Pinto, Pedro: 65
Lopez de Santa Anna, Antonio: 155, 188
Lopez Velarde, Ramon: 189
Loreto Chapel: 183
Los Morenos: 73
Los Naturales Chapel: 10, 13, 14, 15

M

Magno Colegio de San Pedro y San Pablo: 10
Main Cemetery: 155
Main Square: 9
Maldonado, Antonio: 14, 103, 117, 153, 155
Maldonado, Pedro: 15, 107
Margil de Jesus, Antonio (Northern Pilgrim): 10
Marquez de Orozco, Juan: 107
Martinez y Virgili, Antonio: 165
Martinez, Francisco: 99
Martin, Francisco: 55
Maza, Francisco de la: 55
Meade, Mercedes: 81
Medina Vargas Machuca,

Cristobal de: 55
Mena, Pedro de: 81
Mendoza, Viceroy Antonio de: 9, 65,
Mercado, Father Pedro: 10
Mexican Society of Geography and Statistics: 173
Mexican Throne: 125
Mexico: 187, 188
Ministry of Defense, Archives of the: 91
Miranda, Beatriz de: 99
Monte Serrato, Virgin of: 79
Montero, Juan: 121
Morante, Baltazar: 73
Moya de Contreras, Pedro: 91
Muñon, Dr. Sancho: 9
Muriel, Josefina: 83, 129
Muzquiz, Melchor, Count of Regla: 155

N

Nadal y Lluvet, Jacinta: 117
National Art Museum: 155
National Institute of Fine Arts:121
National Library: 65
Navarro Pastrana, Juan: 103
Nava, Manuel de: 131
Notary Archives: 87, 121
Nuestra Señora de la Aurora: 14
Nuestra Señora de las Mercedes Convent: 73ss
Nuestra Señora de las Tres Necesidades Altarpiece: 85
Nuestra Señora de Belem: 149
Nuñez de Haro y Peralta, Archbishop Alonso: 155

O

Ocampo, Salvador de: 73
Oidores Street: 10
Ojea, Hernando de: 55
Oliva de Villaseñor, Juana: 117
Olmedo, Bartolome de: 65
Orejel, Ignacio: 55
Orozco y Berra, Manuel: 131
Orozco y Berra Map Library: 17
Ortiz Cortes, Fernando : 169
Our Lady of, El Refugio: 125
Our Lady of Montserrat: 79

P

Paz, Agustin de: 183
Paris, Alonso: 14
Patriotica School: 169
Peña, Ignacio de la: 125
Peralta, Catalina de: 121
Pereyns, Simon de: 55
Perez de Castañeda, Alonso: 153, 183
Petronila, Jeronima: 153
Pino Suarez Street: 153
Pinos, Mateo de: 16
Plaza y Jaen, Don Cristobal de la: 15
Prendimiento Altarpiece: 131
Presentacion Altarpiece: 131
Puebla: 9

Puebla Chapel: 55
Purisima Concepcion: 13, 87
Purisima Concepcion Chapel: 13, 111

Q

Quintana, Detective Valente: 85

R

Ramirez de Aparicio, Manuel: 17
Ramirez de Contreras, Laureano: 161
Ramirez, Pedro: 13
Real de Naturales Hospital: 165ss
Reforma Avenue: 119
Refugio Street: 125
Regina Convent: 83, 107
Requena, Pedro de: 55, 87
Retes y Largache, Juan de: 107
Rio, Martin del: 117
Rivera, Diego: 95
Rivera, Juan de Dios: 129
Rivera, Miguel Jose de: 16, 65
Robles, Antonio de: 15, 73
Rodriguez de Vado, Alonso: 171
Rodriguez, Diego: 65
Rodriguez, Lorenzo: 55, 161
Rojas, Juan de: 16, 65, 81, 87, 95, 107
Romero Rubio, Manuel: 161
Rosario Chapel: 55
Ruiz Parra, Miguel: 14
Ruiz, Juan: 131

S

Saenz de Izaguirre, Tiburcio: 95, 107
Salazar, Basilio: 13
Salcedo de Espinosa, Juan: 117
San Agustin Convent:: 9, 10, 81, 183, 65
San Agustin Church: 9, 65
San Alejo: 81
San Andres Novitiate: 155
San Andres and Santa Paula Hospital: 155ss
San Angel town: 155
San Antonio Chapel: 16
San Bernardo Convent: 83, 107ss.
San Carlos Academy: 81
San Fernando Convent: 10, 15,17
San Francisco: 155
San Francisco de Mexico Convent:: 9, 10, 173
San Francisco Church: 9, 13, 14
San Francisco Street:: 13
San Francisco, sculpture of: 13
San Gregorio School: 11, 183
San Hipolito Hospital: 149, 151
San Ignacio College: 151
San Ildefonso College: 183
San Ildefonso: 65
San Jeronimo Altarpiece: 131
San Jeronimo Convent: 84
San Jose Chapel: 16, 73
San Jose de Gracia Convent: 83, 103ss.
San Jose de los Españoles Chapel: 15

San Jose de los Naturales Chapel: 16
San Juan de Dios Order: 149
San Juan de la Penitencia Convent: 83, 117ss.
San Juan de Letran: 165, 181,
San Juan de Letran Street: 145
San Lazaro Neighborhood: 73
San Lorenzo Altarpiece: 131
San Lorenzo Convent: 83, 131ss.
San Lorenzo Church: 131
San Pablo College: 11, 183
San Pablo Church: 107
San Pascual Bailon: 85
San Pedro y San Pablo Schools: 11
San Ramon College: 181ss.
San Ramon Street: 181
San Sebastian Hermitage: 10
San Sebastian Street: 10
Sanchez Talaya, Juan: 55
Sanchez, Diego: 79
Sanchez, Hernan: 65
Sanchez, Father Pedro: 10
Santa Ana Novitiate: 155
Santa Brigida Convent: 83, 145ss
Santa Catalina Altarpiece: 16
Santa Catalina de Siena Convent: 83, 135ss.
Santa Cecilia, oil painting of: 65
Santa Clara Convent: 83, 111ss., 121
Santa Ines Convent: 83, 97ss.
Santa Isabel Cloister: 83
Santa Isabel Convent: 121ss.
Santa Maria, Blas de la: 73
Santa Maria de la Caridad College: 177
Santa Monica de Puebla Convent: 85
Santa Paula Cemetery: 155
Santa Rosa de Lima Altarpiece: 131
Santa Teresa La Antigua Convent: 83
Santa Teresa La Nueva Convent: 83
Santo Despedimento Altarpiece: 14
Santo Domingo Church: 9
Santo Domingo Convent: 9, 10
Santos Justo y Pastor: 81
Saviour, Order of the: 145
Santos, Jose de los: 16
Sayago, Jose Joaquin de: 65, 121, 153
School of Commerce: 173
School of Medicine: 171
Senate Chamber: 155
Señor de Burgos Chapel: 10
Serrano, Juan: 131
Servitas Chapel: 10, 16
Siguenza y Gongora, Carlos de: 91, 183
Sobrarias, Marco Antonio: 15
Society of Jesus: 125
Soriano, Neapolitan advocation of Santo Domingo: 10
Spain: 187

T

Talaya, Gines: 55
Tabernacle: 65
Tecto, Juan de: 9
Tepotzotlan: 16, 55
Tepotzotlan Museum: 161
Tercer Orden Chapel: 10, 15, 16, 55, 65, 73
Tercer Orden de San Francisco Chapel: 14
Terceros Hospital: 173ss
Texas: 10
Tlatelolco: 11, 13
Totolapan Christ: 10
Tolsa, Manuel: 81, 183
Torquemada, Brother Juan de: 11, 13
Torres, Lazaro de: 73
Toussaint, Manuel: 131

U

United States: 188
University of Texas: 16
Ureña, Felipe de: 16, 177
Urrutia, Aureliano: 119
Uruguay Street: 181

V

Valverde, Diego de: 65
Vasconcelos, Jose: 95, 183, 189
Velazco, Antonio: 107
Velazco, Diego de: 103
Velazco Viceroy, Luis de: 9, 103
Velazco, Manuel de: 55, 95, 99, 107, 121, 131, 161
Venustiano Carranza Avenue: 16
Vera, Juan de: 73
Vergara, Nicolas de: 87
Vetancourt, Agustin de: 13
Vetancourt, Pedro de San Jose: 161
Viacrucis Chapels: 15
Viceregal Pinacotheca of San Diego: 81, 65
Vidal de Fuentes, Pedro: 121
Villaseca, Alonso de: 183
Villalpando, Cristobal de: 81, 107
Villalpando, Carlos de: 161
Villegas Estate: 173
Villegas, Fernando de: 103
Vitoria, Juan: 79

W

Western Paradise: 91

Y

Yanhuitlan, Oaxaca: 55

Z

Zaldivar Mendoza, Maria: 131
Zaldivar, Ana: 171
Zuleta Street: 16
Zuleta, Pedro de: 10, 13
Zuleta Chapel: 10
Zumaya, Manuel de: 55
Zuñiga, Francisco: 169
Zurbaran: 79

The Printing of, The City of Palaces:
chronicle of a lost heritage,
volume II
was finished on September 20, 1990,
by Hindy's, Hong Kong,
under the supervision of
Jinno International of New York, U.S.A., for
Espejo de Obsidiana, Ediciones, S.A. de C.V.,
Nebraska 170, colonia Napoles,
Delegacion Benito Juarez, 03810 Mexico, D.F.
The edition was supervised by:
Kieran Maule Redmond and Adriana Arrieta Munguia

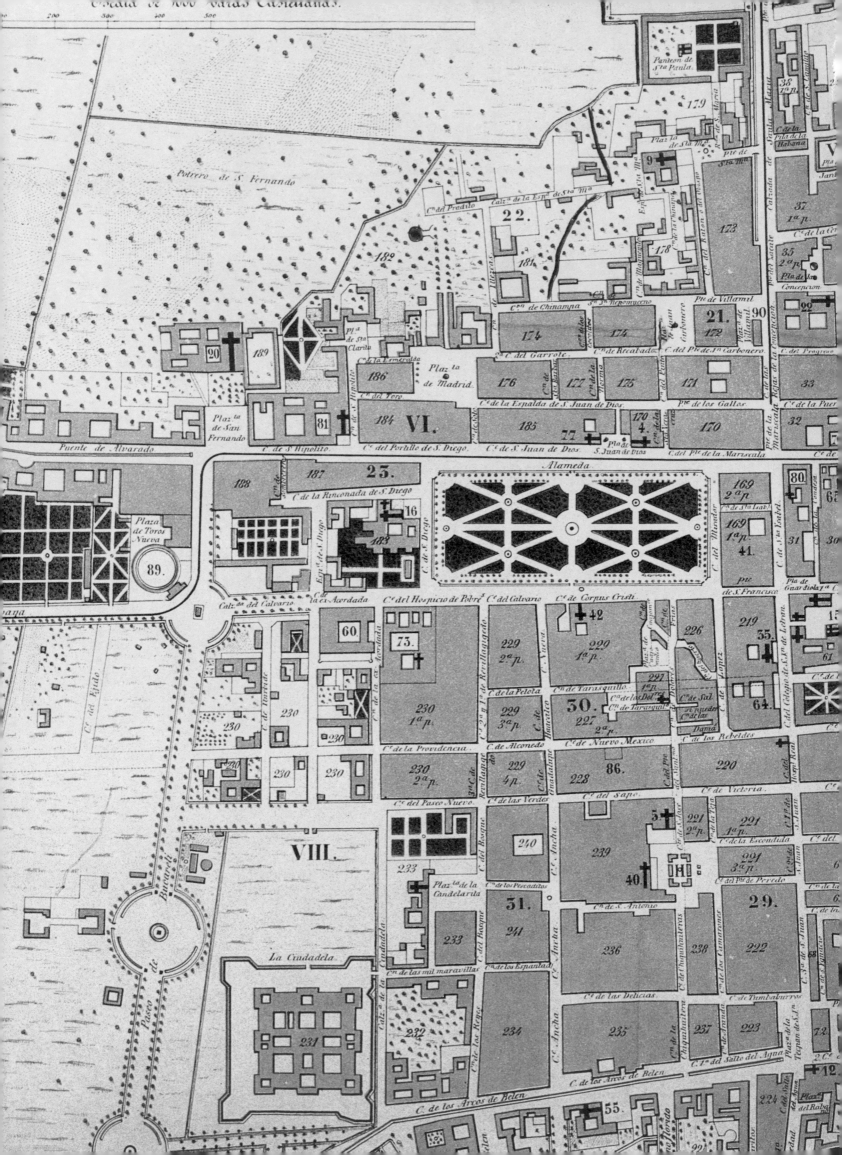